The Way of Karate

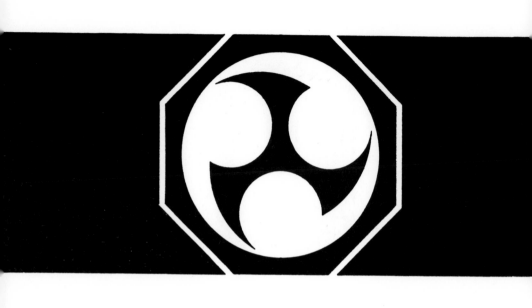

George E. Mattson

The Way of Karate

Rutland, Vermont: CHARLES E. TUTTLE COMPANY: Tokyo, Japan

Published by the Charles E. Tuttle Company, Inc.
of Rutland, Vermont & Tokyo, Japan
with editorial offices at
2-6 Suido 1-chome, Bunkyo-ku, Tokyo 112

LCC Card No. 62-14116
ISBN No. 0-8048-1852-5

First edition, 1963
First paperback edition, 1992
Second printing, 1993

PRINTED IN JAPAN

■ *Dedicated to*
the Okinawan Karate Association
and to the memory of
Mr. Kanei Uechi, Sr.

Contents

Acknowledgments

For their efforts and their assistance in making this book materialize from an idea into a reality, I wish to acknowledge my thanks, particularly...

– to Barbara Peterson, Marjory Otterson, and Mrs. Donald B. Connors for their critical reading of the preliminary drafts.

– to Dr. Amiya Chakravarty, Professor of Comparative Oriental Religions and Literature at Boston University, for contributing the Foreword.

– to Dr. Marvin Solit, specialist in posture problems, for his contribution of "Karate and Health," which he wrote after spending many hours studying training methods at the Mattson Karate-do Academy.

– to Alan Hershdorfer for his skill and patience in taking the karate photographs that make up the bulk of the illustrations.

– to Thomas Bruno, Charles Coughlan, and Donald Mac-Calmon, instructors at the Mattson Karate-do Academy, for their time and skill in posing for many of the photographs.

– to Donald Connors for the use of his photographs of Chinese statues.

– to all Okinawans who so willingly gave of their time and experience in teaching me the art of karate and instilling in me the true spirit of the art. I am in this regard especially grateful to my immediate teacher, Mr. Ryuko Tomose, and to the headmaster of the Uechi Karate Association, Mr. Kanei Uechi.

– to all my other friends who so unselfishly helped and preferred to remain unnamed.

G. E. M.

Foreword

by Dr. Amiya Chakravarty

Karate means "empty hand"—the hand the instrument of the body; the body the instrument of the will. The aim is to develop a synergism of the will, the nerves, and the muscles which manifests itself in the maximum possible controlled release of energy. This munificent efflux is greater than is commonly suspected.

An intriguing quality of karate which is similar to other techniques for self-discipline is the necessity of having to simultaneously develop command of the mind and body. The will has to be disciplined and illuminated in its expression through the medium of the body. The body, receiving this existential efflux, is facilitated in its attainment of the highest well-being. This potential then becomes available to others.

If the training of one is neglected for the other, we will fail in the achievement of the maximum and lose valuable derivations from the process. But even such an uneven disciplining will reveal some of the profound processes that are necessary in the release of the potential through the conscious co-ordination of the manifold unity of the being. Thus, though these processes are dimly perceived, they feed back to the various levels of the mind and body to facilitate the proceeding phases in discipline.

In *The Way of Karate* the author takes up the main traditions and practices of this Okinawan form of physical and mental discipline, which has rightly attracted increasing attention in recent years. The author does not, however, separate calisthenics from its original meaning (in Greek): that of combined strength and beauty. Beauty in the present context would include, as in antiquity, the element of grace or graciousness, which transcends the mere exercise of strength. The excellence and uniqueness of George E. Mattson's book lies in the fact that he lays down the whole science and art of karate in the most exact and demonstrable way with the help of accurate descriptions, the most impressive diagrams and photographs, and interpretations of the precise skills that have to be developed.

He never forgets the essential meaning of karate. He does not offer substitutional methods which would allow either the mind, grace, soul sequence (if we can use such an expression), or the sequence of physical training in techniques to dominate or replace the correlatives on the "other side." The author thus avoids what in yoga terminology in ancient India was described as the yoga *samkat* or the yoga crisis.

The "crisis" lies precisely in neglecting the basic purpose of the psycho-physical training. Although we need the alert body to ward off danger and to conquer attacks from the outside and within, we would be making a sorry bargain if we used the repertoire of physical discipline for the sole purpose of muscle-flexing, showing off, or—even worse—violent, unprovoked use of skills for the harm of our fellow beings.

The yoga sutras of India equally spurn the so-called miraculous mental powers, etc., that may easily become the objective of the lesser yogi who has fallen from his highest prerogative. We can, of course, make use of physical and mental powers for enhancement along partial lines of purposiveness, but it must be remembered that the whole significance and purpose of yoga, as well as of Zen and karate, lies in the enhancement of the entire person and his spiritual nature.

Mr. Mattson gives a fine summation of the historical background of karate, though many details of the history are still unavailable to us. Nearly five thousand years ago, legend states, India had already cultivated mental and physical powers for "weaponless defense." The doctrine of ahimsa is ancient, and it was always allied to the positive use of nonviolent warfare for conquering the opponent and even for his conversion to a state of social sanity. These techniques were seemingly being experimented with in select communities of Hindus and, later on, in Buddhist groups in India.

Bodhidharma (Daruma in Japanese), a Buddhist monk, as the author tells us, studied the Buddhist techniques in India and later went to China, where he taught lay groups and eventually monastic groups at the Shaolin-szu (Shorin-ji in Japanese), a temple in Honan Province. There, it seems, Daruma instituted his "weaponless defense" techniques along with the Buddhist training.

There must have been other monks—contemporaries and those of an earlier date—who were engaged in similar practices based on Taoist and other ancient Chinese traditions; but China has always insisted that the Indian form of thought control, body control, and such other techniques of yogic nonviolence were superior to their Chinese counterparts. It would be exciting to know of mutations similar to those that took place, such as the usually accepted adaptive changes that made the original Dhyana of India become Ch'an in China and later Zen in Japan. One feels sure that these mutational factors always reveal not merely changes in one order of theory or practice but changes in the introduction of new elements and actually of transformations as new civilizations and traditions impinged upon the earlier forms, as in the case of Zen. The whole world of karate, from that viewpoint, would be an Okinawan contribution, even though ideas and techniques originally came from near and far neighbors. Now it is the turn of the near and far Asian neighbors of Okinawa to learn karate, and this applies as well to the other countries and civilizations outside of Asia.

Contemporary civilization needs this new and old view of "power" which the individual can deploy for self-protection and mutual protection when violence has intervened. Karate is not entirely based on nonviolence, but its clear emphasis is on physical resourcefulness without dependence on weapons. It *is* the cultivation of "empty-handedness," allowing the whole body and the mental energy to be devoted in a single-pointed way, though operating through different movements, toward resisting violence without the intention of destroying the opponent. Rather, the force that the opponent uses in an aggressive way can be turned against him by the karate practitioner.

An important distinction has to be drawn at this point between karate-sho, jujitsu karate, and karate-do. Jujitsu karate, whatever its limited importance may be, is a mere technique, like wrestling or boxing, completely divorced from the ontological and ethical philosophy that lies deep in the roots of karate-do. Karate-sho practitioners are devoted mainly to the spectacular physical skills (breaking boards, killing animals, etc.).

Karate-do, however, is built on the harmonized mind and body linked up with the creative and regenerative forces of life. Karate-do is the way of karate, and the author describes it as "the way the universe works" and "the means of attaining the true meaning of life." Evidently, the author draws our attention to the positive side of a skill and discipline which is meant to heal and not to destroy or harm a society.

He knows that the karate skills acquired by a practitioner can be used in the wrong way, as any skill can be, but he also knows that in that case the practitioner will fail. The resources of an evil practitioner will become banal if he reduces karate (or Zen or yoga) to a device that lacks the inwardness of a superior training. As Mr. Mattson points out, self-defense abilities come unconsciously and intuitively after concise, precise, and sustained rational and physical effort. The person of integrity can make the best use of the self-defense and other skillful techniques of karate.

The book is a marvelous presentation of karate-do in its shining depth as well as in its well-proved usefulness. The book is timely because we need now, as never before, the spiritual and mental poles which could give power and relevance to our physical selves. We are under the great pressure of mechanization that thwarts the fresh flow of our physical and mental resources. The way of karate helps us to recover ourselves. This book appears during a period of renewed crises that are apt to confuse and paralyze our body and will, and it provides us with a detailed and spiritual view of the real nature of man's indomitable personality.

■ 1

Introduction

■ What is karate?

Karate (pronounced "car-ah-tay") is the Oriental art and science of self-defense. The practitioners of karate use no artificial weapons for their unusual methods of defense. Instead, they develop the natural weapons of their bodies—feet, hands, elbows, etc.—into silent, hidden weapons that respond with lightning-like speed when necessary.

Karate is founded on scientific principles of body movements that develop the karate devotee into a healthy, well co-ordinated person, both physically and mentally. The Chinese karate masters considered karate to be an extension of their religion. The Okinawan karate masters considered it to be a way of life.

Karate was introduced in Okinawa as a means of self-defense for people who had no weapons. Its usefulness as a method of self-defense decreased as time went on, but increased as a system of physical conditioning. Karate became so popular, in fact, that schools began teaching it in their physical education classes.

Today karate is becoming popular as a sport. The keen reflexes of the karate practitioner are so accurate that he is able to spar with another karate student without using protective equipment.

While karate is the ultimate in weaponless self-defense, its main usefulness and direction today is in its all-encompassing physical, mental, and moral growth—namely, the conditioning process used to develop keen reflexes, excellent co-ordination, and an over-all healthy body.

KANEI UECHI. *Okinawan karate master Uechi is president and head master of the Uechi-ryu Karate Association.*

■ What karate is not

Because karate is so difficult to explain fully and correctly, many proponents of the art tend to over-simplify their explanation and description of karate. This would not be so bad, except that these explanations are usually false or misleading.

In the Orient, karate is respected because people understand what it is. Here in America, men who have studied karate for a short time and do not understand the real meaning of the art demonstrate its spectacular aspects, such as board breaking. This is something that any person can do with little training. People who see this type of exhibition believe it to be the end-all of karate. Other "experts" sell to the public a conglomeration of self-defense tricks which they label karate but which in reality is anything but karate. America is not the only country that has misguided "experts." Even China, the motherland of karate, has had her misinformed proponents.

A karate teacher in China who was known to have the strongest "chop" in the whole country challenged another karate teacher from the "feel of the human mind" style of karate to a fight. The second teacher

GEORGE E. MATTSON. *Author Matt-son, who practices the Okinawan style of karate, is head of the Matt-son Karate-do Academy in Brook-line, Massachusetts.*

tried to talk his way out of the fight but to no avail. The first became so persistent that the second could do nothing but defend himself.

The second teacher knew of the first's ability to break more boards and bricks than any other man in China, so during the ensuing fight he kept away from the first until he found an opening.

The first teacher rushed the second teacher but for an instant left his head unguarded. The second teacher took advantage of this opening by kicking the first teacher on the chin, knocking him down. The first teacher begged for mercy as he lay on the ground. The second took pity on him and let him up. As the first teacher got up from the ground he asked the victor how he could have beaten him when he could break more boards than anyone in China.

The second teacher laughed and said: "You fool! Do you think I am a pile of silent and immovable boards? I am a human being, capable of movement and strategy. After a few months anyone can break boards, but karate skill is not that easy to attain."

The second teacher, now seventy-five years old, is living in Canton, China.

■ Methods of studying karate

Karate is an expression used to describe the "empty-handed" system of self-defense founded in the Orient. Most people fail to realize, however, that there are different approaches used in studying this system.

Karate-sho ("sho" is from English "show") is the showy style of karate that teaches only the spectacular aspects of this art. The proponents of this type of karate display their talents simply as a show.

Jujitsu-karate, or crooked karate, as it is called in the Orient, consists of some self-defense movements taken from the real karate. Because there is no foundation for this system, it has been proved to be inferior even to judo, which is considered to be a sport.

Karate-do is karate as it was taught in China and is now being taught in Okinawa. Karate-do is the "way" of karate as a concept of life. The individual desiring to learn about the attitudes and philosophy of the Orient will find it possible through the study of karate-do. In karate-do there are no short cuts; there are no easy methods. The person must truly want to learn, and he must study hard.

I do not wish to mislead you into believing that it is possible to become an expert at karate-do by reading a book. If you follow the guidance of this book carefully, however, you will be able to learn what karate-do is, and you will learn much about the training. This is all any book on karate can hope to do.

Throughout this book the word karate will be used to mean karate-do.

■ What is meant by the "way"?

The "way" symbolizes the path in which something is accomplished. It is the way the universe works. In karate the way represents the means of attaining the true meaning of life through the path of karate training. The way of karate is not an easy way. It is difficult beyond all expectation. Yet when it is carried through to its rewarding experience of self-mastery, it is beautiful beyond all expectation.

The path of training and discipline developed in karate-do does not end in the training hall. You must live the karate way in order to experience its fullest rewards. Karate-do is not merely an expression of defense or attack. It is, rather, an expression of life lived 24 hours a day, 365 days a year. Indeed, the way of karate is a philosophy of life—a rich, rewarding philosophy if carried through, past the boundaries of obvious self-defense techniques, into the realm of mind-searching discipline.

The obvious is plain; it is simple. The obvious can be learned by all. The intuitive is hidden. The intuitive must be sought out, nurtured, and developed. Karate-do has been likened to an oak seed. Within the seed is the potential of a huge tree if it is properly cared for. Within karate-do is the potential of a new person: a person huge in all the capabilities that will make him respected and confident. It is here for you to nurture, study, and restudy.

■ History of karate to date

The first thing that every new student of karate learns is the unique history of karate. It is unique because of the way it has been handed down through the centuries. There were no books written about it, and the only way a student learned was to listen carefully while his instructor repeated what *his* instructor had told him when he first started. I will now simply repeat what my instructor told me.

Approximately 5,000 years ago there lived in India a rich prince who developed the first crude version of weaponless self-defense. This prince watched the movements of the animals and studied their methods of defense. He noted the stealth the tiger used before successfully killing its prey. He studied how the birds of the forest fought, noting their wing and foot movements. The prince applied these fighting techniques to the human body and found that many of them could be successfully employed.

The prince then experimented on slaves to discover the weak points of the human body. He did this quite successfully by jabbing needles into the body of a slave until a puncture resulted in the slave's death. Legend states that over one hundred slaves were used in this bizarre experiment. All of the pressure points and weak points of the human body were found. The prince used the fighting techniques of the animals and directed them to the weak points of the human

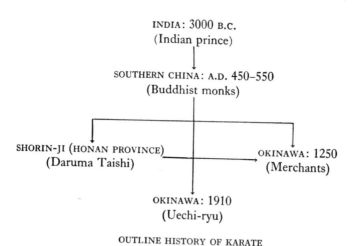

INDIA: 3000 B.C.
(Indian prince)

SOUTHERN CHINA: A.D. 450–550
(Buddhist monks)

SHORIN-JI (HONAN PROVINCE)
(Daruma Taishi)

OKINAWA: 1250
(Merchants)

OKINAWA: 1910
(Uechi-ryu)

OUTLINE HISTORY OF KARATE

body in formulating his weaponless method of self-defense.

The next figure of importance in karate's history was Bodhidharma, known to the Japanese as Daruma Taishi. He gave to karate the most important contribution it ever received: the spirit of Zen. Bodhidharma, a Buddhist monk, studied Buddhism in India. It is possible that he also received instruction in self-defense in India. During his time there were many thieves who would rob and kill a traveler for his money, whether he was a peasant or a Buddhist monk. Since the monks were not allowed to carry weapons, they were taught self-defense at their monasteries along with Buddhism.

Bodhidharma went to China to teach at the Shaolin-szu (Shorin-ji in Japanese), a temple in Honan Province. There he found the Chinese people unable to grasp the complicated esthetic Indian style of Buddhism, so he taught a natural, more easily understood religion: Zen Buddhism. Even though the Zen doctrine was simpler than Indian Buddhism, the Chinese peasants still found it difficult to comprehend. The mental exercises used in Zen proved to be too difficult. The peasants tired of the exercises and found their minds constantly wandering. Bodhidharma then instituted a system of self-defense exercises that would condition their bodies so that they could better experience the Zen "enlightenment."

Ordinary exercises did not work because they conditioned the body but had no effect on the mind.

Bodhidharma devised a series of movements that, when done nearly perfectly, would give the performer the experience of enlightenment. Once he accomplished this and knew within himself what enlightenment was, he could apply or practice this feeling in his everyday life. Even though this exercise was designed mainly to give the experience of enlightenment to the Zen practitioner, it came to be the foundation of the Chinese *ch'uan-fa* (literally "fist way"), which the Japanese call *kempo,* as we shall refer to it from here on. The exercise came to be called by different names, and because of its seemingly simple and meaningless movements, it eventually came to be disregarded by the majority of later karate proponents.

Fortunately, a few of the Chinese masters recognized and understood the importance of this exercise. As time passed, however, Zen and karate became less and less associated. These few masters passed the exercise on to their students, telling them that it should never be altered or left out of a training session. They told their students that this exercise was the foundation of karate, although seldom did they explain why. The masters believed that the student should experience the importance of it within himself and not be told why it was so important. If the student was told, he would take the exercise for granted, but if he experienced it on his own, the impression would be greater.

In modern-day karate, many schools recognize the need of Zen in the movements and even go so far as to tell their students what parts of Zen are the most important, but they fail to give a practical method of attaining these principles. Knowing that karate is performed with a mind that is completely aware yet is thoughtless (i.e., thought-free) and nongrasping is fine, but you cannot attain this thoughtlessness by *thinking* that your mind should be thoughtless. Knowing that your body should focus all of its power into a thrust, a kick, or a strike is one of the main principles that make karate effective. But how is this accomplished while the mind is clear and not thinking about this focus?

The section on karate and Zen will go into these principles at greater length. I do not expect you to be able to apply these principles simply by reading about them, but I do want you to become familiar with them so that when you finally experience them you will know how to apply the experience to karate.

The exercise that Bodhidharma invented was passed down in its original form and shaped the foundations of the Chinese style of kempo known as *pangai-noon*. In 1900 Mr. Uechi, an Okinawan, went to southern China and studied the three foremost styles of kempo. He studied for ten years under one of the greatest kempo masters living at that time. At the end of the ten years Mr. Uechi took the best *kata* (formal exercises) from the three styles. From the pangai-noon style itself, he retained the exercise that Bodhidharma developed: the exercise called *sanchin*. From the pangai-noon and the other two styles, he adapted the *kata* of *seisan* and *san-ju-roku (san-shih-liu* in Chinese). These three kata became the foundation for the famous Uechi-ryu Karate Association in Okinawa, a member of the Okinawan Karate Association.

You will be able to experience the Zen principles used in karate when you have become proficient at sanchin. Once you have experienced these principles, collectively called the "third eye," you will be able to apply them practically to your karate techniques.

When Bodhidharma first introduced his third-eye developing exercise to his students, he told them something that I consider to be extremely important, both in karate and in life:

"Spirit and body shall be inseparably united. Because you are so overcome with the demands of your bodies, you seem unable to comprehend the benevolence of mind-body unity. I am therefore going to give you a doctrine; train your body and mind with it so that you may attain a higher perception."

■ The Okinawan sai and its connection with karate

About 400 years ago, Japan began to assert control over the island of Okinawa. One of the edicts forced the Okinawan people to turn over their weapons to the Japanese. One of these weapons was the *sai*.

The sai was a three-pronged weapon used both for defense and attack (similar to a sword) and for

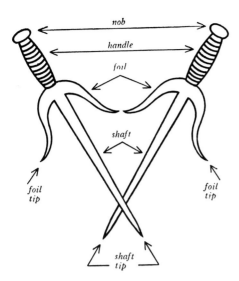

nob

handle

foil

shaft

foil
tip

foil
tip

shaft
tip

CROSSED SAI. *Techniques for using the Okinawan sai formed the basis for the development of karate techniques of defense and attack.*

throwing (similar to a spear). The sai masters carried three of these weapons. Two were held in the hands, the shaft extending the length of the forearm and the nub hidden in the hand. The third sai was hooked in the belt as an extra in case one should be lost while fighting or in case one was thrown. There were sai masters who were able to pin a man's foot to the ground with the foil tip of the sai.

The sai was extremely effective against a club or a samurai sword attack. The foil would hook the sword, and with a powerful twist of the wrist, the master could snap the sword in two. The nub of the sai was used for striking in the counterattack, or a downward strike with the shaft of the sai could be used.

The strengthened forearm (developed through the arm-strengthening exercise) replaced the shaft of the sai for deflecting attacks from clubs. The karate blocks replaced the foil of the sai for hooking and thwarting attacks. The strengthened fingers replaced the tip of the sai, and the hardened foreknuckle replaced the nub.

During the period when the sai was used in Okinawa, a student perfected sai techniques by training with kata similar in nature to those used by karate students. Today, karate has completely replaced the sai, but at the Uechi-ryu school the crossed sai are displayed as a symbol of their significance in karate's unique history.

■ Karate and Buddhism in Chinese art

Statues of Buddha are sometimes accompanied by statues of his karate monk guards, who are shown standing or sitting to either side of him. They are always portrayed in an important karate stance or arm position.

One of the guards, usually the one to the right of Buddha, is in a "soft" or relaxed state, while the guard to the left of Buddha is shown in a "hard" or focused state. After karate's introduction into Zen Buddhism by Bodhidharma, the monks studying Zen in China also studied karate. Bodhidharma believed that mind-body training was much more desirable than either strict mental or strict physical training.

Very little was written about karate as it pertained to Zen Buddhism. Most of what was written concealed the fact that karate was taught as a part of Zen Buddhist training, although all the statues and paintings of this period that pertained to Zen Buddhism contained elements of karate. The artists of this period depicted qualities of Zen Buddhism with the help of karate expressions and positions. It is important to realize at this point that the principles of Zen Buddhism were not unique to Zen alone but were practiced many years before in the form of Taoism, lamaism, quietism, hedonism, and other mysterious religions or philosophies of the past. Zen merely took the most desirable qualities of all these religions and developed what was called Zen Buddhism. It is important to understand something of the methods of these other religions in order to understand Zen Buddhism fully.

From Taoism, the quality of harmony with nature is found. We must not fight the fundamental laws of nature, but yield to them. The Tao or way is the symbol of Taoism; it represents the unspeakable means by which man is integrated with the universe. Weakness and softness represent the Tao. To grasp is to lose; to yield is to conquer.

Quietism arose from a belief that man could, through a form of self-hypnosis, make himself into a better person. This method of stilling one's senses

BUDDHA AND MONK GUARDS. *Statues of Buddha are sometimes accompanied by statues of monk guards portrayed in important karate stances or arm positions.*

was similar in nature to yoga. Instead of remaining in a sitting position while attaining this state, the Chinese used "strange exercises of the limbs, stretching, and postures" (as told by Chuang Tzu). This form of active meditation seems to be quite similar in nature to that used by Bodhidharma. Quite possibly that passage referred to Bodhidharma, since at that time distinctions between various branches of religion were at best hazy.

In nearly all of the religions of India and China, especially Buddhism, Taoism, and Confucianism, many of the important principles and doctrines overlap. One of the points they all had in common was their secret techniques of attaining *siddhi,* enlightenment, *hsin, kung,* etc., that formed the foundation of their religion. Many times, in the statues, paintings, or scriptures of the time, reference would be made to these secret techniques, but in a way that would convey a double meaning. To the uninitiated, the reference would have an exoteric meaning, but to

BUDDHA. *Everything in karate can be traced to some principle of Zen, which derived, through Bodhidharma, from the original teachings of Buddha.*

the initiated it would be a sign that showed the viewer or reader that the author was one of the cult.

It was not uncommon for the various religious sects to make war on one another, and therefore these secret techniques, which in reality were techniques of self-defense as well as techniques of their religious instructions, had to be closely guarded. Instruction was carried on within the walls of the monasteries, and the members were sworn to secrecy. The only records of these techniques were the statues and paintings of the period. Without knowledge of karate, even these signs were misinterpreted.

The picture on page 27 represents Indian Buddhism with its karate contribution. The Indian Buddha in the center represents Indian Buddhism as it was introduced to China. The two karate-monk guards represent the secret karate techniques used during this period in connection with Buddhism.

The guards in this picture are standing with their arms in two variations of the closed-gate position. While in this stance the monks could meditate and still be able to defend themselves if necessary. The

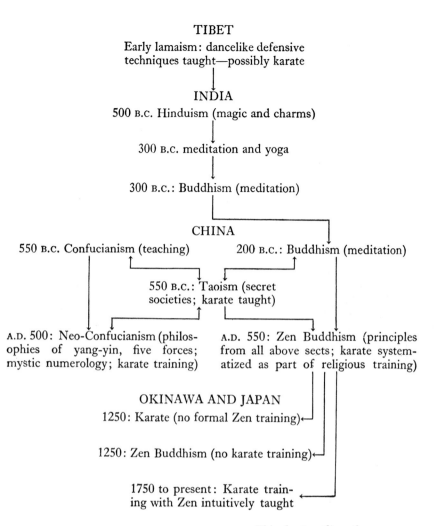

TIBET
Early lamaism: dancelike defensive
techniques taught—possibly karate

INDIA
500 B.C. Hinduism (magic and charms)

300 B.C. meditation and yoga

300 B.C.: Buddhism (meditation)

CHINA
550 B.C. Confucianism (teaching)   200 B.C.: Buddhism (meditation)

550 B.C.: Taoism (secret
societies; karate taught)

A.D. 500: Neo-Confucianism (philos-   A.D. 550: Zen Buddhism (principles
ophies of yang-yin, five forces;   from all above sects; karate system-
mystic numerology; karate training)   atized as part of religious training)

OKINAWA AND JAPAN
1250: Karate (no formal Zen training)

1250: Zen Buddhism (no karate training)

1750 to present: Karate training with Zen intuitively taught

KARATE IN HISTORICAL PERSPECTIVE. *This chart outlines the
flow of karate through various Indian and Chinese religious
and philosophical sects.*

closed-gate position shown by the guard to the right
of Buddha is the same closed-gate position sanchin
ends with. The guard to the left of Buddha is shown
in a closed-gate position that bears close resemblance
to a Christian praying position. Whenever the karate
monks were meditating, they assumed a karate stance.
When walking, they would have their hands in a closed-
gate position for safety. People who did not understand this accepted the exoteric meaning of the pos-

GUARDIAN DEITY. *Evidence of self-defense techniques among ancient religious sects can often be found in statues portraying their gods and holy men.*

ture and believed the hand position had something to do with their meditation. A more detailed examination of the "hard-soft" philosophy represented by the two karate guards is given in the introduction to sanchin.

At some period in Chinese history, karate became popular more as a means of protection than as a part of Buddhism. When this happened, both Buddhism and karate lost part of their essence. When the Buddhist monks found that they did not have to protect themselves any longer because the people accepted them as holy men, they gradually came to disregard the karate training, even though the training had a twofold purpose.

The Zen Buddhism that was taught from that time on was no longer strict Indian Buddhism nor Chinese Zen Buddhism but a modification of both. The attainment of enlightenment through meditation was again the most accepted method, but the down-to-earth Chinese philosophy remained. In this form, Zen Buddhism was introduced to other countries.

■ **Karate and Zen**

Everything done in karate—every movement, every

feeling—can be traced to some principle of Zen. A student overlooking this fact misses the lifeblood of karate.

The factor that makes karate different from Zen is that Zen is practiced as a religion. Karate uses the principles of Zen to help perfect the self-defense movements and mind-body co-ordination involved in this art. The principles of Zen, beautiful in themselves, are used in karate with one idea in mind: making the body into an efficient, well co-ordinated unit. This unit works in such a manner that terms like body and mind are no longer applicable. The mind and body become as one, working together. Once this harmonious interaction of the mind and body is accomplished, karate will help you in life—provided you practice what you learn!

You will find some of the following principles difficult to understand when you first acquaint yourself with karate. This difficulty does not exist because the principles are wrong, but because these principles are new to you. Do not be disappointed if you are unable to apply them within a few months or even within a few years. Instead, familiarize yourself with them frequently and use them for goals.

1. KARATE SPIRIT

Undoubtedly one of the most important factors needed to become really good at karate is the very basic karate spirit. This is the determination and courage displayed in every movement performed; without this sense of determination, the karate movements become empty, frail, and lifeless. Keep in mind that this spirit cannot be attained until the actual movements become mind-body reactions; that is, until the movements can be performed without having the feeling of "I am doing it."

2. MU-SHIN (NO-MINDEDNESS)

The principle of *mu-shin* is the ability to clear your mind of all thoughts. At first this may seem a bit strange and purposeless. Upon closer analysis, however, you will find it quite the contrary. When a person attempts to see something very clearly, he usually does just the opposite of what he should do to see it clearly and wholly. He will, in all probability, try to look at it very hard and closely. He will look at the object as though he were trying to see through it. The harder he looks, the less he sees.

The Zen master does not look at an object. He lets the object gaze at him. He does not attempt to see the object with his eyes or his mind, nor does he try to focus the object in his mind. Instead he clears his mind completely and allows the object to reflect itself to him. He does not need to look hard at it to bring it into his mind. *He sees more by looking softer.*

How can this principle be used in karate? First, by realizing that the harder you concentrate or "look" at your opponent, the less you will see of him. To see your opponent in his entirety, you must see him as he really exists. He is not an arm, a leg, a thrust, or a kick. This man is an infinite combination of techniques and the possessor of an unlimited amount of strategy. He is human and therefore possesses all the limitations, fears, and weaknesses of our species. To look at your opponent in any other way would weaken your own position. To see your opponent this way, you must clear your mind of all thoughts of self-defense or of techniques. *Gaze into his eyes and see all.* Because you are completely aware in this state, your actions will be taken over by your mind-body directed reflexes. You will not make mistakes when this state is reached.

3. NONINTERRUPTION

The principle of noninterruption is very important and is difficult to perfect. Simply stated, it means that your defense should begin when your opponent's attack begins. This does not mean that your arm begins to move when your opponent's arm begins to move. The defense referred to here is the mental defense or co-ordination of your body's reflexes, so that when the defense becomes physical, your body's defenses will react like a triggered gun. Watching a karate master block a thrust makes an observer think that the defense is slow or interrupted. This is not the case, however; the master simply delays his physical defense until the right moment. Because his defensive movement is a reaction and is extremely fast, he will be able to block an attack, even though the attack is half completed before he begins his defense.

You may ask yourself at this point: "Would I not be swinging at everything that came in my path if my reactions were developed to this point? Would I have any control over my reflexes?"

If you were to simply develop self-defense reflexes for the sake of adequate self-defense, I would have to say that you will not have too good control over your reflexes. A playful tap on the shoulder could be disastrous to the jester. The person who develops animalistic defensive movements (which is what karate movements are) without the mind training or discipline can be *extremely dangerous* both to himself and to others. How would a person feel if he used the dangerous self-defense techniques on a person whom he should not have used them on? He could very easily kill or maim him for life, simply because he had preconceived thoughts about the circumstances or the situation. He would see everyone as an aggressor, and he could deal with him in only one way.

This animalistic instinct is the very thing we wish to control. The karate student who uses the principle of noninterruption does not react on preconceived thoughts of defense or attack. He deals with each situation differently, according to what his senses reflect to him, not what he "thinks" the situation calls for. A hand on the shoulder does not necessarily mean an act of aggression. A playful tap on the shoulder will not provoke the student into hitting the jester.

The karate student always remains "aware" of what is taking place around him, and he is always alert. Because he sees people and things differently than most people do, he will not be confused as easily by foreign situations. *Not only do you see more of what you are looking at, but you see it more as it really exists.*

4. EFFORTLESSNESS

The principle of effortlessness corresponds closely with the others. In fact, each principle in karate overlaps another. To know one thoroughly, you must know all of the principles. The ability to perform a movement as described in noninterruption, and to do this without "thinking through" the movement, is, in essence, what effortlessness means.

Here again, you must condition your eyes to perceive an action and your mind to reflect this action to your mind-body directed reflexes. Do not attempt to think out a movement before performing it in karate. In other words, do not say to yourself: "I must block this thrust with a rising block." If you must think out an action in this manner, it will be ineffective.

The principles just developed for you are basic. You may eventually come by them on your own by studying karate, but it would take many, many years. Just knowing what the principles are is not going to help you use them, but knowing what they are and being able to experience them in the Zen kata, sanchin, will help you greatly in attempting to perfect karate.

Do not try to grasp your opponent's movements. Whether they are simulated (as in karate sparring) or real, let the movements reflect themselves to your mind-body directed reflexes. With much practice, these reflexes will react with less and less interruption, and they will be performed with more and more spirit.

The movements must be learned well before you can attempt to direct them with mind-body reflexes. This takes a long time. Do not become discouraged at what you believe to be slow progress. Karate is not something you learn in ten quick and easy lessons.

The longer you study, the more you will realize there is much to learn. Because karate is so challenging, it should never become boring. When you get to be ninety, your interest will still be as great as it was when you received your first promotion.

I will close this section with a quotation by the great Bodhidharma. It was spoken in reference to the doctrine of Buddhism, but I feel that it holds true of karate also:

"It can be comprehended only after a long hard discipline and by enduring what is most difficult to endure, and by practicing what is most difficult to practice. Men of inferior virtue and wisdom are not allowed to understand anything about it. All the labors of such ones will come to naught."

■ Karate attitude

In studying karate under the guidance of the Okinawan masters, one cannot help noticing the way the master acts while he is in the training hall and while he is leading his normal everyday life. His manner appears calm and easy, and one can sense a great difference from the Western way of life. The Zen master possesses this same attitude.

Karate attitude is the over-all manner of the karate master. This attitude or manner covers all phases of the master's life—with his family, with his friends, or with his students. Unlike the Western manner (changeable to suit the occasion), the karate master's attitude is a natural one, unchanging and unchangeable. To better understand this attitude, let us examine a few of its characteristics.

1. HUMILITY

To best understand the humility possessed by the karate masters, we must attempt to understand what this humility is like. The Westerner considers humility a matter of simply being without pride or self-assertion. He recognizes in the karate master this type of humility, but I believe wrongly so. If this definition of humility were correct, we could speak of anyone not deserving of respect as being humble, as long as he didn't have pride. This, however, we do not do. Only those people who have accomplished something great and are deserving of respect can be humble. Only those Westerners who have every right to be proud, yet contain their pride, are said to be humble.

The karate masters possess a great amount of pride in a form that appears like humility. They know within themselves their tremendous accomplishments, yet they never lose sight of their tremendous shortcomings. The hard-soft law of karate applies even here: the combination of extremes to form the ideal blend. With this blend, the karate masters will talk with their newest student with sincerity and humility as long as the student's attitude is right. Should the student become demanding or sarcastic, the master will walk away silently.

2. THE ABSENCE OF PRECONCEIVED THOUGHTS

Although mentioned previously in connection with a Zen principle, the absence of preconceived thoughts warrants mention again in respect to the karate master's attitude. Whenever a master talks or deals with people, he does so with no preconceived thoughts about the other person or the dealings. He does not attempt to categorize the person into something that he is not. The master's association with people is a beautiful one, because he deals with them with an open mind. He does not make friends easily, for the master does not want to have his feelings hurt at a later date by an untrue friend. Rather than this, he takes a long time to accept the person as his friend, but once he does, the person is his friend for life.

3. SELF-CONFIDENCE

The master's life is filled with self-confidence. The people he associates with sense this confidence and trust in his judgments. The master does not make snap decisions but analyzes the problem before coming to a conclusion. Once the decision has been made, he accepts it as being the right decision for the moment, subject to change.

The master accepts the world as it is, knowing that life is not always soft and easy. He knows that tomorrow he may be dead or that some other catastrophe may occur. This does not prevent him from enjoying life today, for he knows that no matter how much he worries, tomorrow, with all its hardships or happiness, will come, no matter how he feels.

The master accepts life as the willow tree accepts the wind. Rather than fight the inevitable by being immovable as the oak tree, the willow will bend, not suffering any hardships, whereas the oak will fight and fight and in the end be destroyed by its own stubbornness.

When strife comes, fight it, but do not become bitter and hard because of it. Remember that the world is constantly changing and that you must change with the world. Tomorrow after the wind has calmed, the willow will bounce back to its original straightness, whereas the oak will have the unhealable scars of the day before.

■2
Karate Terminology

The karate terminology used in this book is the same as that used in Okinawa. Because karate should be practiced as it is practiced there, this terminology is very important for the proper atmosphere. When you refer to a foot-strike, a thrust, or any other karate technique, always use the correct term for the movement or the technique. During the workout, while you are learning the terms, say each one aloud as you perform the movement that it represents. In this way you will learn the terms quickly.

Japanese vowels are pronounced as in Spanish or Italian, each being given approximately its full value. This includes the terminal *e* in such words as *karate, kumite, mae, and semete*. Consonants are much as in English, except that *g* is always hard.

TERM	EXPLANATION (*where applicable*)
mu-shin	no-mindedness
noninterruption	
kime	focus
academy	training hall
kiai	shout of spirit
karate-ka	karate student
kata	formal exercise
waza	technique
tsuki	thrust
uchi	strike
uke	block
keri (or geri)	foot-strike
jodan	upper area
chudan	middle area

gedan	lower area
uchi	inner (50%) block
soto	outer (75%) block
semete	assailant
ukete	defender
musubi-dachi	neutral stance
sanchin-dachi	dynamic tension stance
kiba-dachi	low stance (horse stance)
hachiji-dachi	informal stance
zenkutsu-dachi	leaning-forward stance
neko-ashi-dachi	cat's-foot stance
kihon kumite	fundamental sparring
yakusoku kumite	prearranged sparring
jiyu kumite	free-style sparring
keri-waza	foot-striking techniques

Striking parts of the leg:

koshi	ball of foot
sokuto	edge of foot
kakato	heel
teisoku	sole
hittsui	knee

Other terms used to designate a foot-strike:

geri	strike
mae	front
yoko	side
ushiro	back

Foot-striking terms as used in the workout:

keri-waza	foot-striking techniques
mae-geri-keage	front-snap foot-strike
mae-geri-kekomi	front foot-thrust
yoko-geri-keage	side-snap foot-strike
yoko-geri-kekomi	side foot-thrust
ushiro-geri-kekomi	back foot-thrust
mae-tobi-geri	flying front foot-strike
hittsui-geri	knee-strike
uke-waza	blocking techniques

Parts of arm and hand used for blocking, striking, and thrusting:

seiken	fore-fist
ude	arm
riken	back-fist
tettsui	bottom fist
hiraken	foreknuckle fist

ipponken	one-knuckle fist
yonhon-nukite	spear hand
shuto	knife hand
haito	ridge hand
haishu	back hand
teisho	palm hand
kakuto	bent wrist
empi	elbow

Terms used in the workout:

uke-waza	blocking techniques
chudan-uke	middle-area block
chudan-soto-uke	outside (75%) middle-area block
chudan-uchi-uke	inside (50%) middle-area block
kake-uke	hooking block
gedan-barai	downward block
jodan-age-uke	upper rising block

Other blocks shown in the kata, exercises, or techniques:

tsuki-uke	thrusting block (used in seisan)
keito-uke	wrist block 1 (used in exercises)
kakuto-uke	wrist block 2 (used in exercises)
juji-uke	X block (used in seisan)
mawashi-uke	circular block (used in sanchin)
nagashi-uke	pushing block (used in yakusoku kumite)
haishu-uke	hand-heel block (used in exercises)

Thrusting techniques as used in the workout:

choku-zuki	forefist straight thrust
jodan-zuki	upper straight thrust
chudan-zuki	middle straight thrust
gedan-zuki	low straight thrust

Striking techniques as used in the workout:

haito-uchi	ridge-hand strike (used in seisan)
empi-uchi	elbow-strike (used in exercises and seisan)
tate-empi-uchi	vertical elbow-strike

yoko-empi-uchi	side elbow-strike
ushiro-empi-uchi	rear elbow-strike
riken-uchi	back-fist strike (used in seisan)
shuto-uchi	knife-hand strike (used in seisan)

The striking techniques listed above are those most frequently used. Many more striking techniques may be learned through the study of the kata. To learn the terms quickly, say each of them aloud as you perform the technique. Continue this procedure until the terms are learned.

▪ 3

Karate Stretching Exercises

The karate stretching exercises are an excellent method of loosening up properly before beginning the more formal karate training. All of the exercises are designed to stretch and loosen, not to strengthen or to harden. In karate one makes maximum use of those muscles which he uses in everyday life. This requires that every inch of the body be in perfect condition.

Perform these exercises every day before training with the other techniques.

▪ Heel pivot exercise

Relax the pivoting leg completely. Throw the foot as far to the side as possible. Repeat four times, then do on other side. Do 10 repetitions on each side.

▪ Foot-and-leg twist

The exercise begins with the foot twisting in a circular motion, pivoting at the ankle. After two or three turns, the size of the circle increases until the foot and ankle are twisting in a circular path, pivoting at the knee. When the circle is at its largest, stop and retrace the circular path, making it smaller and smaller. At the completion of the circle, foot-strike out (front-snap foot-strike). Change legs and repeat the exercise.

■ Knee circular bend

Keep your feet flat on the floor and together throughout this exercise. Your back and head remain as straight as possible. Complete two circular paths to the left, then push your legs back straight twice. Then repeat the exercise to the right. Do about 10 repetitions of the exercise to both sides.

■ Waist "scoop"

This exercise should be learned in steps. Later, when it has been memorized, begin co-ordinating the parts until finally the whole exercise can be performed smoothly.

a. Stand straight, feet together, hands and arms in position shown.

b. Fall forward at the waist. Do not pull yourself down, but relax your stomach and fall forward.

c. Scoop upward in a circular path. Keep your arms in the same position throughout the exercise. Continue the upward movement of your body until you are standing nearly straight. Then fall down at the waist again, retracing the path previously taken.▶

■ Trunk-stretching exercise

Place your hands in a closed-gate position (left hand over right fist) and raise arms as high over head as possible, keeping back and head straight. Relax your body (keeping legs straight) and fall to the rear. Rotate in a circular motion as shown in the pictures.

▸Stop when you reach the position shown in *d*. (Arms, however, are still as they are in *a*.)

   d. Bring your arms to the position shown.

   e. Relax your body and fall forward at the waist. Keeping your legs straight, touch the floor to your left with your fists. Then return to position *d*.

   f. Relax your body and fall forward, touching the floor to your right.

   g, h. Standing straight, inhale deeply while expanding your arms and chest as shown. Exhale by retracing the path taken by your arms and slowly exhaling at the same time. Consciously relax your whole body during the inhalation and exhalation of breath.

■ Leg lift and turn exercise

This exercise develops body co-ordination and stability. Keep yourself as straight and as relaxed as possible throughout the movements.

a. Stand straight, feet together.

b. Raise left leg as shown.

c. Extend leg as shown in this side-view picture.

d. Keeping your body facing forward, rotate your leg to the left side. Bend the supporting leg at the knee for balance. Keep your other leg straight, toes pointing outward. Retrace the motion, bringing your leg to the front again, and then return to position shown in *b,* then *a*.

Repeat the exercise with your right leg. Do about 10 repetitions of this exercise with each leg.

■ Double arm-thrusting exercise

This exercise, like all karate exercises, stresses good posture and good karate form throughout the

movements. In perfecting these exercises, the karate student perfects his karate techniques.

a. Get into a good left sanchin position, arms in a double ready-thrust position.

b. Extend arms fully, turning them smoothly from a palm-up position to a palm-down position. Exhale as you extend the arms.

c. Focus as you squeeze your hands into a fist. Your wrist remains straight while you squeeze your hands. (Note: Do not focus until your form is nearly perfect. The focus will be developed in the kata, sanchin.)

d. Relax completely. Inhale deeply as you return your arms to a double ready-thrust position. Turn hands smoothly from a palm-down to a palm-up position.

e. Extend your arms to the side. Exhale as arms are being extended. Again the palms of your hands turn from a palm-up to a palm-down position.

f. Focus (for advanced students) as you squeeze your hands into fists.

g. Inhale as you return to double ready-thrust position.

h. Exhale as you thrust downward. Arm-turning technique same as above.

i. Focus (for advanced students) as you squeeze hands into fists.

NOTE: Keep your body in a good posture at all times. Keep your shoulders back and down. Repeat exercise about 10 times.

■ Wrist-blocking exercise

In this exercise, four different methods of blocking are developed. Learn the exercise well, for it is extremely important

a. Strike outward, keeping your shoulders back and down, your fingers straight, thumbs tucked in, your elbows in, and in general keep good karate posture. (Advanced students focus at point of impact.)

b. Strike inward. Keep fingers straight and shoulders back and down. Do not touch wrists by moving arms too close. (Advanced students focus at point of impact.)

c. Strike upward, fingers pointing downward. Arms are parallel.

d. Strike downward, fingers pointing upward.

Repeat exercise about 15 times, varying the speed with which movements are made.

■ Fishtail-blocking exercise

This exercise is a variation of the wrist-blocking exercise. It is useful because it stretches and strengthens the wrists.

a. Strike to the left. The outside of your left wrist and the inside of your right wrist are the striking surface. Continue the movement until your right wrist is in line with your left side. Keep your forearms parallel.

b. Strike to the right, using your outside right wrist and inside left wrist as the striking agent. In making the movement, do not move your fingers first,

but move just the arms, keeping the finger tips still until the arms and hands are in the proper position. Then the whole arm finishes the movement. Continue the movement until your left wrist is in line with your right side. Repeat this series of movements about 20 times, varying the speed.

c. At a signal from your instructor, do two focused blocks. (Focus at the farthest point.) Bring your arms to the position shown.

d. Do a double thrusting block. Return your arms to position *c.*

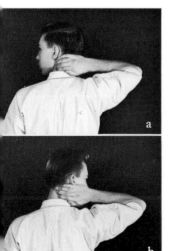

■ **Neck-massaging exercise**

This exercise will help stretch your neck and upper back muscles. Remember to remain relaxed throughout the movements and to keep your posture correct.

a. Grasp the left side of your neck with your right hand. Your head is turned away from your extended elbow.

b. Slowly turn your head toward the elbow. As you do so, pull your neck muscles gently toward the center of your body.

Repeat the exercise 10 times to each side. Remember, while performing the exercise, to lift the back of your head as high as possible in order to straighten and lengthen your spine. Tuck your chin in.

■ Straight-leg striking exercise

This exercise stretches those muscles that will make your foot-strikes more perfect. Keep your upper body *motionless* throughout the movements and, more important, keep your back, neck, and head straight.

a. Strike to the rear with your *straight* left leg. *Do not move your upper body!* Return the leg to begining position—namely, the left foot parallel to the right.

b. Strike to the side with the side of your left foot. Point the toes of your left foot *down and in.* Do not sacrifice form for height.

c. After returning to the beginning position, strike to the front, touching your left hand. Return to beginning position. (Picture shows side view.) Strike again to the front, but this time aim for the *outside* of the right hand.

Repeat this exercise 10 times with each leg.

ELBOW-STRIKING EXERCISE

■ **Side-stretching exercise**

While doing this exercise, keep your whole body relaxed and in a good posture.

a. Fall to your right side, pivoting at your waist. Do not move your lower body. Let the weight of your left arm stretch the muscles of your side.

b. Repeat the exercise to the left.

Do 10 repetitions of this exercise to each side.

■ **Elbow-striking exercise**

This exercise develops all of the elbow techniques used in karate. In addition, it is an excellent exercise in itself.

a. Assume a good right sanchin stance. Block with your left arm (chudan-uke).

b. Strike upward with your right elbow, pointing your finger tips down and forward. (Tighten the forearm.) Counteract the arm movement by withdrawing your left arm into a ready-thrust position (front vertical elbow-strike: tate-empi-uchi).

c. In a circular motion, draw your right hand across your chest as shown, keeping the arm in close to your body. Strike to the side with your elbow.

d. Completed side elbow-strike (yoko-empi-uchi).

e. Extend your right arm to the front. (Arm is in a sanchin position.)

f. Strike to the rear (ko-empi-uchi). Keep shoulders back and down throughout the exercise.

To continue exercise, block with the *right* arm. Repeat the exercise, using your left arm instead of the right. Do about 10 repetitions with each arm.

■ Front leg-stretching exercise

Keep your rear leg straight and fully extended. Relax your body completely, especially your waist and thighs. Balance yourself with your hands. Rock back and forth, stretching the Achilles tendon of your rear leg. Bounce up and down, stretching the muscle in your upper leg. Keep your back straight and tuck your chin in.

■ Sitting leg-stretching exercise

a. Sit with your back and head straight. Place feet together and draw them in as close as possible to your body. Grasp ankles with your hands.

b. Place elbows on knees. Bend forward with your body, pushing legs to the floor. It is important that you remain completely relaxed during the movements.

Repeat this exercise 10 times.

■ **Deep-breathing exercise**

This last exercise stretches the whole upper body and relaxes it.

a. Beginning position.

b. Inhale as you extend the arms upward in a circular path. Exhale as you return the arms to position *a.*

▪4

Formal Karate Training: Preliminaries

▪ The ceremonial bow

The purpose of the bowing ceremony is to separate the exercises from the formal workout. Bowing is the traditional symbol of mutual respect in the Orient. In the class bow, the students and the instructor show their mutual respect by bowing together.

The bow is begun by sitting in an erect manner with back and neck straight, as shown in *a*. Hands are placed on thighs. At a signal from the instructor, the whole class bows by placing their hands about 12 inches in front of their knees, as shown in *b* and *c*. Keeping their heads and backs in a straight line, they bend over until their elbows touch the floor. They remain in this position for two seconds; then, at a signal from the instructor, the whole class returns to the sitting position shown in *a*.

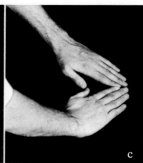

■ Student-to-student bow

The standing bow is performed before every karate technique except those techniques which are repeated over and over for training or learning purposes. When one student is training with another student, and a bow is to be performed, the students bow together, each keeping his eyes focused on the other's eyes. As long as both students bow equally low and together, a good bow can be done. The hand position is left over right. Hands are crossed, but the thumbs are not interlocked.

You do not take your eyes off another student's eyes for the purpose of safety. The new student may forget to bow and at the signal to bow may immediately begin his attacking technique, thus endangering the other person. The crossed hands protect the groin during this bow.

■ Student-to-instructor bow (left)

Because the instructor's abilities warrant confidence within the student, the student performs a regular bow to the instructor whenever a bow is called for. The instructor, however, must not lower his eyes during the bow.

■ Posture-correcting stance

The Chinese knew the importance of good posture. Therefore, whenever a new student was accepted for training, he would spend his first year and a half doing nothing but developing a good body structure and posture. After the year and a half, the kempo master would begin teaching the students kempo techniques and kata.

The corrective procedure is called the Four Levels of the Horse. The first level (opposite page) is the hardest and must be perfected before going on to the higher levels, which are not shown in this book. The purpose of this training is to develop the bone structure strong and straight. Without this training, strong muscles will not be used to their maximum efficiency.

■ Training schedule

a. Maintain the horse-level position until the muscles of the body become cramped. For the first week or so, you will probably not be able to stay in this position longer than three minutes, if the stance is done correctly.

b. Practice the stance every day until it can be done comfortably for one hour. After a year and a half of this training, your body will have developed a solid bone formation, good posture and structure, and very flexible muscles. The desired muscles should be as soft as cotton when relaxed and as tight as steel when flexed. The combination of soft-hard, relaxed-focus, gives the karate student the ability to move as fast as lightning and to focus his movements, using all of the concentrated power of his body.

■ Training aids

The illustration shows the correct position for horse level one. The front view shows the correct front position. Note that the legs form a structure similar to that of a house. If the lower leg is bent too far to the side, the structure will be weak and collapse. The bones of the body serve a purpose similar to that of the frame of a house. If the frame is weak and lopsided, no matter how much material is placed around it, the house will still be weak.

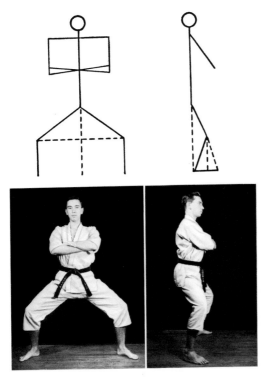

POSTURE-CORRECTING STANCE. *Horse level one is the first and most difficult step of the Chinese posture-correcting procedure called the Four Levels of the Horse.*

The side view shows the correct side position. The knees should never tilt forward more than one-half the length of the foot. The triangle formed by the foot and the knee should be an isosceles triangle. The head, neck, and back form a straight line, even with the back of the feet.

■ **Important training points**

a. Remember the purposes of the horse stance level one:

(1) To develop a good bone structure.

(2) To develop a correct posture.

(3) To develop flexible and "soft" muscles.

(4) To develop the power of concentration and perception.

b. How to attain a good stance.

(1) Get into a good stance, correcting yourself in front of a mirror. Or have someone else correct you.

(2) Straighten your head by raising the back of your head and by tilting it to the rear until it is straight with your back.

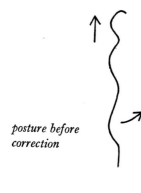

posture before correction

posture after correction

(3) Straighten your back by tucking your pelvis under and forward until your back is straight, as shown in the illustration.

(4) Check posture with pictures and diagrams to insure correctness.

c. Breathing and relaxing.

(1) You will find that if you have to force your body into this correct stance and have to strain yourself to stay in this position you will tire after one minute. DO NOT stay in this stance longer than your body can comfortably assume it. Perfection can only be attained after many months or years of practice.

(2) Keep your body relaxed and free from any tension. Breathe deeply and normally, As soon as you find your body tensing and becoming cramped, stop for at least a couple of hours before trying the stance again. The longer you practice this level of the horse, the longer you will be able to stay in the stance at one time, comfortable and relaxed.

(3) Look straight ahead. Focus your eyes on a spot and hold it.

■ **Introduction to the kata (formal exercises)**

A kata, or formal exercise, is a series of prearranged movements that develop specific abilities in the practitioner. There are three fundamental kata in Uechi's style of karate. Sanchin, the most important of these, develops the principles of Zen that are the foundation for true karate. Sanchin also develops basic physical principles that are essential for the finest karate.

Seisan, the second kata, develops actual defensive and counterattacking techniques that become mind-body reactions when the kata is perfected. The better the kata is performed, the better are the mind-body reactions developed.

San-ju-roku is the most advanced kata in Uechi's style of karate. In it, the student develops advanced defensive and counterattacking techniques that become mind-body reactions as the kata is perfected. This kata will not be shown in this book because of its complexity.

The principles of Zen and the physical principles that are developed in sanchin are applied to the techniques of the kata seisan and san-ju-roku.

Sanchin enables the student to develop muscular

control, giving him the ability to focus his techniques at the correct moment for maximum power and to relax his muscles completely for maximum speed. The focus is developed so that the student can apply it without having to think out the action in his mind.

The kata are an excellent way to practice karate techniques by yourself. It is advisable to practice in front of a mirror so that you may correct mistakes in form as they occur.

∎ 5

Sanchin: Formal Exercise I

∎ What is sanchin?

Sanchin (pronounced "sahn-cheen") is the formal exercise or series of prearranged movements developed by Bodhidharma. This exercise, a form of *active meditation*, gives the practitioner the experience that a Zen master obtains through strict mental discipline when the form is brought to a high degree of perfection.

The student, when performing an advanced or highly developed sanchin, controls every muscle of his body while moving that body in a smooth, prearranged pattern. This muscular control or discipline is accomplished by "soft" and "hard" movements performed while the body is in perfect postural postions. The soft movements are performed while the muscles are soft and relaxed. These movements are the ones in which speed is necessary. The hard movements, called focuses, represent the complete tensing of the muscles. This concentrated force gives the movement maximum power. This focus in sanchin, when prolonged, is called dynamic tension.

When the practitioner has learned the kata movements to a high degree of accuracy, performing the complete kata soft, he then begins the focusing and dynamic-tension training. When he can perform the kata as it is supposed to be executed with a high degree of proficiency, he will reach the state of sanchin in which his body is completely "aware" and his mind acts only as a reflector, not having to think out the body's actions. When the student reaches this stage, his body and mind act as they are in nature: *as one*.

Every action performed while in this state is a mind-body reaction.

Sanchin gives a person who is not a Zen master the ability to acquire the "third eye" or composite of all the Zen principles used in karate. Without sanchin, karate movements are meaningless. The karate masters of China and Okinawa say that sanchin is karate and that karate is sanchin. More will be said about this in the intoduction to seisan.

■ **Physical, psychological, and philosophical principles developed in sanchin**

When a student first begins to study karate, he will only be able to develop the physical principles of karate, such as stance, posture, etc. As he continues his development and continues to perfect the physical movements of karate, he will begin to experience the psychological principles, such as no-mindedness, effortlessness, etc. These two types of principles will aid him greatly in his karate development. He will act with confidence and surety. The longer he studies, the more he will realize karate contains not only a means of self-defense but also a philosophy of life. After many years of training, the student will be able to apply the same techniques which he formerly believed to be merely physical in nature to his daily life. When this occurs, the true nature of karate will appear to the student.

The following are some of the basic and not so basic principles that are developed in sanchin. Upon closer examination and study, the student will be able to uncover many more.

1. THE BASIC KARATE STANCE.

The sanchin stance has been proved to be the most stable stance from all directions.

2. THE BASIC ARM MOVEMENTS.

The sanchin arm position is the finishing position for nearly all of the arm movements performed in karate. A mistake can be readily identified by simply checking the position with its sanchin equivalent.

3. THE BASIC FORWARD COUNTERATTACKING STEP.

The sanchin step develops the ability to move forward while protecting the groin from attack. This crescent-like step is used only when stepping into an

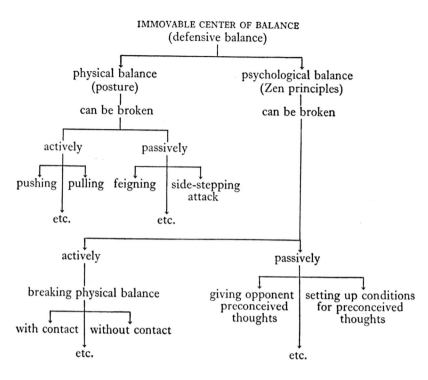

IMMOVABLE CENTER OF BALANCE
(defensive balance)

physical balance (posture) — can be broken

actively — pushing, pulling, etc.

passively — feigning, side-stepping attack, etc.

psychological balance (Zen principles) — can be broken

actively — breaking physical balance — with contact, without contact, etc.

passively — giving opponent preconceived thoughts, setting up conditions for preconceived thoughts, etc.

BREAKING AN OPPONENT'S STABILITY. *This chart summarizes the means by which an opponent's stability—physical or psychological—can be broken.*

attacker's defense zone, or in the zone where your opponent is able to reach your body with an attack.

4. STABILITY.

Sanchin develops in the karate practitioner the ability to maintain an *immovable center of balance.* (In defense, this center of balance is referred to as *defensive balance.*) In defense, two people are attempting to break one another's defensive balance long enough to apply their attacking or counterattacking techniques. Immovable center of balance, or defensive balance, is the combination of physical balance (posture) and psychological balance (Zen principles) in a person participating in self-defense or, if carried to its extreme, in life.

To break an opponent's defense balance, one must in some way upset his center of physical balance or distract his mind so that his psychological balance is broken. Physical balance is broken when you have successfully maneuvered your opponent into a position where his main concern is regaining balance. In other words, one's physical balance is broken when techniques of attack or defense must be abandoned in order to cope with the problem of regaining a suitable position. During this period of upset balance one is vulnerable to the attack of the person who has been able to break his center of physical balance without having to abandon his position of stability.

Physical balance can be broken *actively or passively*. Active breaking of physical balance is accomplished through the application of a technique in which physical contact is necessary, such as pulling your opponent off balance while he is attacking you.

Passive breaking of physical balance is effected through the application of a technique in which physical contact is not necessary, such as feigning an attack in a such manner that your opponent loses his center of physical balance in an attempt to dodge or in any other way avoid the technique.

Psychological balance is broken when you have successfully distracted your opponent's mind into thinking preconceived thoughts that you wish him to think. While his mind is laboring over distracting thoughts, he becomes prey to a successful attack. Only a mind that is completely clear and not thinking thoughts of defense or attack has psychological balance. The degree to which your opponent's psychological balance compares with yours determines the advantage or disadvantage you will have in dealing with him if all other things are equal: health, circumstances, physical balance, etc.

Psychological balance can be broken actively or passively. It can be broken actively by successfully breaking your opponent's physical balance, through physical contact or without it. One cannot maintain psychological balance once his physical balance has been broken. This unexpected occurrence will cause him to redirect his attention to regaining physical balance rather than to contemplation of attack or defense techniques. Passively, your opponent's psychological balance can be broken by causing him to have preconceived thoughts about his dealings with you without breaking his physical balance. If you can change your opponent's mind from a contemplative one to a grasping one, you have succeeded in breaking his psychological balance.

A contemplative mind is a mind that reflects events as they actually occur. This mind is most capable of finding appropriate solutions or counteractions to cope with the situation. A feigned movement will not affect this person's mind so that he will lose his center of balance in an attempt to deflect an attack that in reality does not exist. Rather, this person will only act on what is reflected to him, so that a feigned attack will direct him to change his position enough to make his opponent either continue the attack to a point where a defensive technique will be possible or forget the feigned attack, since no purpose was served by its action.

A grasping mind, however, contains preconceived thoughts about events that in reality exist only in the grasping mind. This person sees the beginning of an attack and immediately "sees" the whole attack in his mind. In other words, this person grasps a complete thought about an uncompleted event. The grasping mind directs an appropriate technique for the preconceived attack. His body directs the technique to the attack, even though the attack was in reality completed *only* in his *own* mind.

Passively, your opponent's psychological balance can be broken by setting up conditions that will give him preconceived thoughts. By appearing as though you were about ready to attack with a foot-strike but actually attacking with a thrust, you will be placing thoughts in your opponent's mind of defensive techniques for foot-strikes. When you do attack, he will be unable to cope with a foot-strike that materializes as a thrust.

Since most people do not possess a contemplative mind, you will find breaking, your opponent's psychological balance most easy. In the few who do possess a truly contemplative mind, your efforts will be in vain, so rather than being concerned with breaking your opponent's psychological balance (which in most cases will be easy), concern yourself with developing a contemplative mind that will defeat your opponent's by its superiority.

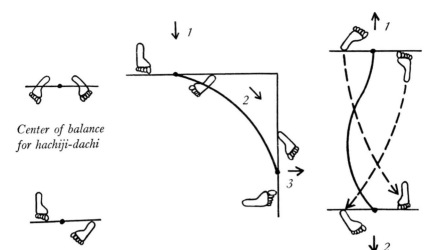

Center of balance
for hachiji-dachi

Center of balance
for sanchin-dachi

Moving center of balance. Arrows show direction body is
facing while standing (1) and
(3) and while moving (2).

Moving center of balance during a 180-degree turn. Arrow
1 shows direction of stance
before turn. Arrow 2 shows
direction after turn.

Physical and psychological balance can be perfected
through the study and application of sanchin.

5. IMMOVABLE CENTER OF BALANCE.

The center of balance of a person performing a
movement or technique is the center weight of his
body, balanced evenly between his feet. When a
person is standing still, whether in a sanchin stance
or any other karate stance, the center of balance is
directly over the center position of the feet.

While one is changing one's position, the center of
balance moves in co-ordination with the feet. Should
one's center of balance be concentrated more on
one leg than on the other, or more to the front than
to the rear, the balance of the body is not centered.
When the balance is not centered, whether the person
is active (moving) or inactive (still), his balance is
most easily disturbed, or moved off balance.

Balance can be disturbed from without (another
person pulling or pushing) or from within (no other
person involved in disturbing your balance). The most
stable center of balance is that balance which is developed from having the entire weight of the body direct-

ed to the area that is centered between moving or still feet.

The most effective way to shift your center of balance as you shift your feet is to fall (your entire body) in the direction of the moving leg. Do not lift the leg to be moved first and then shift weight to the other leg and then push the body to the direction in which you are moving. The center of balance must, in order to be centered, move whenever the legs or upper body moves. The center of balance must then shift with the movement (in the same direction). Should the center of balance remain static when a movement is executed, the person is not in balance.

In karate this immovable center of balance or defensive balance must be present at all times. While moving, your body must possess the stability of a rolling ball, the center of the ball representing your immovable center of balance. While moving, your body must not fight resistance at your opponent's will but must "give" in order to set up conditions ideal to resistance—*for you*.

In other words, do not attempt to break your opponent's balance, block a thrust, or perform some other technique at a moment or point in his attack when the attack is at its strongest. Rather "give" to the resistance, use the time to set up conditions in your favor, and then—when his attack is weakened—spring back with your waiting counterattack. Remember to keep your center of balance strong, confident, and sure at all times.

With a bit of thought, one will be able to see how maintaining an immovable center of balance can be applied to everyday life as well as to self-defense.

6. ABILITY TO FOCUS A MOVEMENT.

Sanchin develops in the student a natural ability to focus an attack or defensive technique. A focus is a concentration of body power into a defensive or counterattacking technique. Your body remains "soft" or relaxed during the delivery of a technique and "hard" or tensed at the completion of the technique. In sanchin you develop this focus so that it can be applied to the rest of your karate techniques naturally, without having to "think" the focus into your movement.

■ **Legend of the three gods of sanchin**

There is a karate legend originating in China that stresses the importance of sanchin. In the Taoist religion of ancient times there were believed to be three mythological gods that were the finest fighters in China. They were only undefeatable, though, when they were fighting together. They were the gods of the eyes, of breathing, and of posture. These same three characteristics are developed in sanchin. Used together, they form an unbeatable combination.

■ **How to learn and study sanchin**

1. BASIC PRINCIPLES

For best results, learn the kata in six steps or stages:

a. Learn the foot movements and turns.

b. Learn the arm movements.

c. Combine the foot and arm movements.

d. When sanchin, part one, has been learned well, study sanchin, part two.

e. Slowly develop the breathing techniques, the focuses, and dynamic tension.

f. Perfect the kata.

Whenever possible, have another karate student watch your kata and make corrections. Go through the movements slowly and stop after each one. Your partner (acting instructor) then corrects your position, using the pictures as a guide. When he feels that you are in a good position, he will nod his head for you to continue.

The student who is performing the kata must not speak during the exercise, and the instructor should use gestures whenever possible in order not to distract the student. Manually correct the arm position rather than tell the student orally what is wrong.

At each workout, you should do at least three sanchin. In the beginning, you will be able to do more because your body remains relaxed throughout the kata. After a couple of months, when you begin to develop the breathing and focusing techniques, three sanchin will prove quite exhausting.

Keep in mind from the beginning that the initial purpose of sanchin is not to develop self-defense techniques but to build the foundation for the other kata.

THE SANCHIN STANCE

Without a strong and well-developed sanchin, your whole karate structure will be weak.

2. THE SANCHIN STANCE

The sanchin stance is the most stable position known from all directions if correctly used. It is extremely strong from the front or rear. You can move from one position to another with speed and without weakening your stance.

Important points to remember about the sanchin stance are the following:

a. Always keep the rear foot straight. Your knee is bent inward slightly.

b. The rear toe is in line with the forward heel. The distance from the heel of the forward foot to the rear toe is slightly more than shoulder width.

c. The forward foot is bent inward at a 40-degree angle. The knee is bent inward slightly.

d. Your body is straight, and the weight is centered within the stance.

e. Make sure that you buttocks are tucked in and are in a straight line with your back. If your posture is poor, you will not be able to change your stance without swaying your body. The upper part of your body should always remain at the same level, not swaying or bobbing up and down. An opponent should not be able to detect forward movement except by watching your feet.

3. THE SANCHIN STEP AND TURN

The crescent step developed in sanchin is used to

THE SANCHIN STEP AND TURN

move forward when facing an opponent. Your groin is protected from a foot-strike while stepping forward to defend yourself or to counterattack. The turn is the quickest and safest way of turning.

The following are important points to remember about the sanchin step and turn:

a. Always straighten the forward foot before moving.

b. As you move, do not sway or bob up and down. Your eyes should never move off their target—your opponent or simply straight ahead.

c. The foot that moves forward stays close to the floor at all times—so close that if a grain of sand were placed between your foot and the floor, your foot would touch it. Do not slide your foot on the floor, however, when you move.

d. When you start your turn, pivot first on the toe of the back foot until it is in such a position that, at the completion of the turn, it will be in a forward position and bent inward at a 40-degree angle. In a circular path, the forward foot moves around and takes its place as the rear foot.

e. Always do the turn slowly in the kata, but practice it fast alone from time to time. In a fast turn, look to the rear as your rear foot pivots and quickly follow through with the forward foot. This allows you to size up the situation and gives you a chance to formulate your defensive technique in time to deflect a thrust or a foot-strike.

4. THE SANCHIN ARM MOVEMENTS

The arm movements in sanchin are designed to develop the student's ability to thrust, block, and focus. The sanchin arm movements also develop in the student the method used in karate to counteract a block or a thrust. The basic sanchin arm position is the strongest position in which you can place your arms to the front. It is the final position for most of your karate blocks and thrusts. Once this position is learned well, you can automatically end up in it after completing a technique.

Important points to remember about the sanchin arm movements:

a. In the basic position, the arms form a 90-degree angle at the elbow. The hands are flat and straight with the arms. Your finger tips are *shoulder high.*

b. Keep your elbows *in.* They should be even with your sides and one fist's width away. Your hand should be pointing out slightly and bent out at the thumbs. *Tuck the thumbs in.*

c. Learn the arm movements first without worrying about your foot movements or stance. Just stand in a comfortable position while learning the technique.

d. First, with your right arm, keep your elbows in close to your sides as you draw the right arm back into a ready-thrust position. Bring the arm back and toward the left arm so that it passes across the left forearm. Continue to draw it back, keeping it close to your body.

e. When in a ready-thrust position, the right arm is parallel to the floor. Your hand is flat and is point-

ing straight out to the front. Your palm is facing upward.

f. The thrust. The outward movement of the arm is called a thrust. The hand is twisted until, at the completion of the thrust, it is in a palm-down position. This same arm movement is used for nearly all karate arm-thrusts.

g. The withdrawal. The arm is brought back to a basic sanchin position after the thrust. The elbow moves downward and in as the hand comes back.

h. Throughout the right-arm movement, the left arm *does not move.*

i. At the completion of the thrust, the arm is at shoulder height and completely straight.

j. At no time during the arm movement do you move your shoulders forward. To stabilize your shoulders, push them back and down at the point of focus.

k. Always practice the arm movements slowly in the kata, but develop speed in the karate thrusting exercise.

5. KARATE BREATHING AS DEVELOPED IN SANCHIN

When the kata is learned well, the student can develop the karate breathing technique. Following is the basic method of karate breathing:

a. When withdrawing the arm to a ready-thrust position, inhale deeply and slowly, pushing the diaphragm down. The only muscles used in breathing are the intercostal muscles of the chest. Breathe slowly, smelling the air. (Whenever you use your sense of smell while breathing, you must be breathing properly. By the same reasoning, when you taste your food while eating, you must be eating properly.)

b. Exhale while the arm is being extended. When the arm is being extended slowly, as in sanchin, exhale slowly. When the arm stops, the exhaling is completed.

c. Inhale when rising; exhale when lowering yourself.

Following is the method of breathing and focusing as used in sanchin:

a. Assuming sanchin stance: focus, or tighten body when movement is completed. Stay that way until position is checked.

b. Relax. Withdraw arm to ready-thrust position. Inhale while performing this movement. Stop inhaling when arm reaches ready-thrust position.

c. Relax still. Thrust out slowly. Exhale slowly eight parts of air in lungs. When arm is fully extended, it still has a slight bend at the elbow. This prevents the arm from being grabbed and broken because of no "give." Focus your whole body into the thrust. At the moment of focus, exhale most of the remaining air with a *kiai.* The kiai (pronounced "key-I") is executed by making a deep-sounded yell (similar to a loud, clearly sounded "hi") that expands the abdomen and tenses the whole body. Most of the air is pushed out of the lungs by the kiai. The remaining air is pushed downward, expanding the abdomen.

d. Relax immediately. Pull the arm slowly back to the original sanchin arm position. Kiai and focus again as your arm reaches the sanchin position.

e. Relax. Move into your next position.

f. Repeat steps.

The controlling of your body through this soft-hard-soft-hard discipline gives it the flexibility and co-ordination that the Chinese and Okinawan masters alone have perfected up to now.

Sanchin is the reason why karate is so effective. The karate strength that appears to an observer to be supernatural is nothing more than an application of sanchin's soft-hard law, which makes a thrust very fast and strong. The short, concentrated effort in the focus puts into action all the power of the body. Sanchin also relieves the tensions in the human body that are built up in daily life.

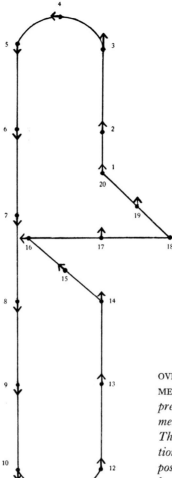

OVER-ALL SANCHIN MOVE-MENT CHART. *This chart presents the over-all movements involved in sanchin. The arrous indicate the direction the body faces at each position. For details see following pages and explanation below.*

■ Sanchin: the complete kata

Now that you are familiar with the basic movements of which sanchin is composed, the next step is to put them together. Follow the diagrams and other aids carefully. Refer to the basic movements often to check for correctness of form.

The chart shows the over-all movements involved in sanchin. Each dot represents your center-of-balance position after completing a step or a turn. The first 13 movements are basic sanchin steps and turns. Numbers 3 to 10 represent the two turns.

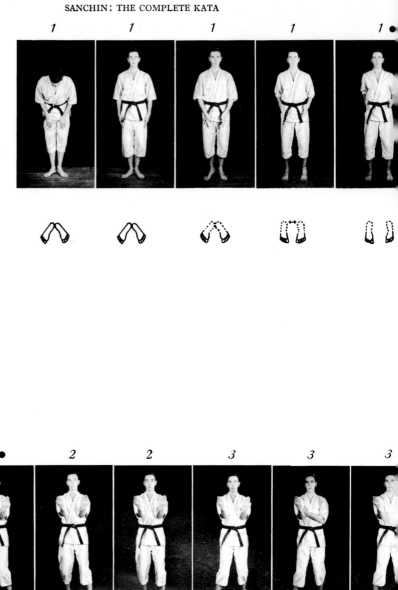

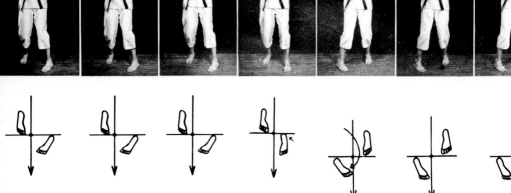

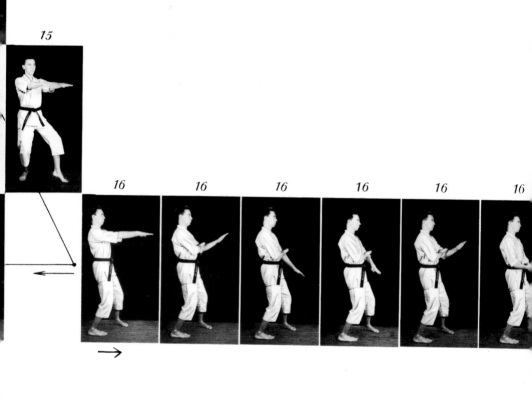

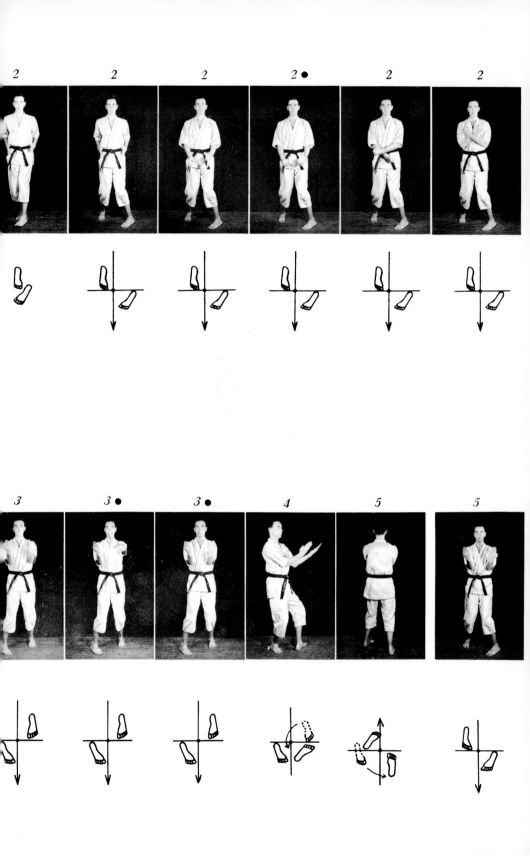

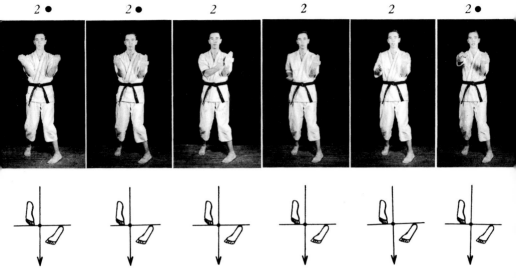

Steps 1 to 5 comprise the basic Sanchin steps included in the first half of the over-all exercise. From step 5 to 14, the beginning of the second part of the Sanchin kata, perform the following steps :

CHART POSITION

5	Perform a right-arm sanchin movement, with focus.
6	Take a sanchin step (moving into a right sanchin stance).
6	Perfom a left-arm sanchin movement.
7	Take a sanchin step (moving into a left sanchin stance).
7	Perform a right-arm sanchin movement.
8	Take a sanchin step (moving into a right sanchin stance).
8	Perform a left-arm sanchin movement.
9	Take a sanchin step (moving into a left sanchin stance).
9	Perform a right-arm sanchin movement.
10	Take a sanchin step (moving into a right sanchin stance).
10	Perform a left-arm sanchin movement.
11-12	Execute a sanchin turn (moving a left sanchin stance.
12	Perform a right-arm sanchin movement.
13	Take a sanchin step (moving into a right sanchin stance).
13	Perform a left-arm sanchin movement.
14	Take a sanchin step (moving into a left sanchin stance).
14	Perform a right-arm sanchin movement.

The rest, the second part, of the sanchin kata is shown on the following pages.

14   14   14   14 ●

Repeat this sequence two more times. Then . . .

14

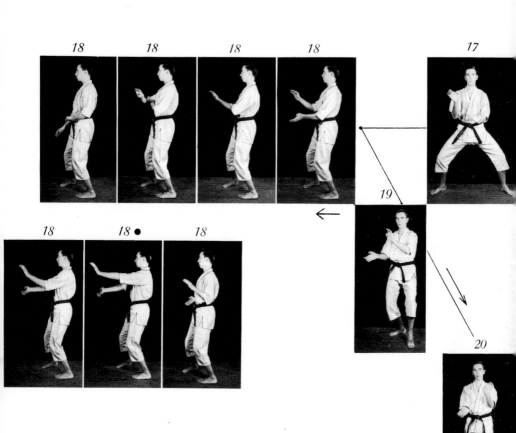

18   18   18   18   17

19

18   18 ●   18

20

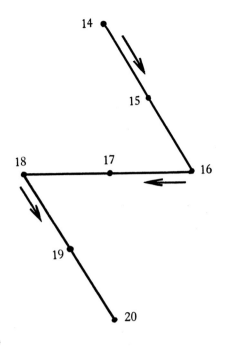

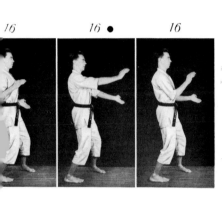

MAWASHI-UKE FOOT-MOVEMENT CHART.
*Heavy dots indicate where movements
were captured by the camera. Numbers
correspond to those of photos and of foot
chart on next page.*

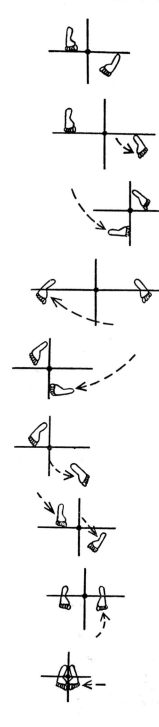

Closing of sanchin's bassic movements. From this position do 3 arm-thrusts. Then . . .

begin turn to side.

First sidestep completed. Do mawashi-uke. Then . . .

begin 180-degree turn.

Second turning step completed. Do mawashi-uke. Then . . .

begin 90-degree turn.

Third and final turning step completed. Do third and final mawashi-uke. Then . . .

return forward foot to a parallel position as your arms go into a closed-gate position. Then . . .

bring left foot toward right and lower your arms to your side. Bow.

Number 14 represents a sliding step to the left. Although the step is performed at a 45-degree angle, your body at the completion of the step is facing 90 degrees from position 13. Number 15 represents a 180-degree "horse-stance" turn. Number 16 represents an angular sliding step to the left front. Upon completion of the last movement, you should be standing in the exact position you started in and facing in the same direction.

The illustrations show first the completed sanchin stance and then the complete kata, parts one and two. Where appropriate, arrows indicate the direction of foot movements. The movements to be focused are indicated by a small black dot, placed above the corresponding picture. All other movements in the sequence are to be performed in a relaxed condition. Learn these basic movements. Then follow the sanchin movement chart to determine when turns should be executed and when sanchin, part two, begins. Study also the mawashi-uke foot-movement chart and the foot chart for sanchin's final three movements. The whole kata is performed slowly and smoothly. Until the kata is learned well, do the movements relaxed *only*.

■ Summary of sanchin

Once again I will stress the importance of sanchin. You must learn it well in order to become really good at karate. You could learn just the self-defense techniques, without the mind training received in sanchin, but you would then not be learning karate-do.

Karate involves much more than knowing a few self-defense techniques and possibly being able to apply them on a slow opponent. Karate involves developing reflexes, co-ordination, attitude, and numerous other principles that, when combined, make an unbeatable combination.

Start off slowly in sanchin. Do not begin the focusing training until your posture is good and the exercise is flawless. The Okinawan masters make their students work on sanchin for nearly three months before they allow them to do anything else. Do not rush into the more spectacular aspects of karate, for in the end you will suffer. Your form will be poor, and your whole karate defense will be weak. Make up your mind from the beginning that you are going to study karate correctly and then stick to your resolution.

You should remember that once you begin your training, you will be able to continue with it the rest of your life. So take your time.

.6

Other Karate Stances

Even though the basic sanchin stance is the best for over-all stability, there are times when you will find other stances that will serve the purpose better. Five of these stances are described here.

■ **Hachiji-dachi (informal stance)**

This stance represents the average stance you assume during the day. Most of your kata and exercises begin with this stance.

■ **Musubi-dachi (neutral stance)**

The stance represents the natural, normal way of standing. It is the most correct way of standing. The kata close in this position.

■ Kiba-dachi (low stance)

This stance is used most effectively when you are in close to your opponent and you wish to counterattack to the body. It is used in all the kata.

The following are important points to remember about the low stance:

1. The advantage of the low stance is that your center of gravity is lowered. Your stability is increased, and you are less likely to get hit while in this stance.

2. Your forward foot is pointing straight ahead or slightly inward.

3. In the low stance (as in the horse-level posture-correcting stance) your forelegs are perpendicular to the floor. If they rest at an angle, your stance will be either too close or too large.

4. Keep your back and head straight.

5. Keep your shoulders in line with your hips.

6. It is difficult to maneuver from this stance, so do not stay in it long. Return quickly to a sanchin stance for maximum mobility.

■ Zenkutsu-dachi (leaning-forward stance)

The leaning-forward stance is found in the kata seisan. It is used in this instance with an elbow-thrust to the solar plexus. The forward momentum of your body is used in this technique along with the upward and outward thrusting motion of the elbow. This stance is very strong to the front but weak to the sides and back. Your ability to maneuver from this stance is weak, so do not stay in it after completing the technique.

Important points to remember about the leaning-forward stance are the following:

1. The rear foot is flat on the floor and is pointing forward.

2. When used with an elbow-thrust, your body and head are in line with your rear leg upon completion of the thrust. This gives the elbow-thrust more momentum, making it more effective.

3. When used with a thrust, your back and head are perpendicular to the floor.

4. The forward leg is perpendicular to the floor.

5. The rear leg is bent slightly at the knee for flexibility and mobility.

■ Neko-ashi-dachi (cat's-foot stance)

The cat's-foot stance is used in san-ju-roku, an advanced kata not shown in this book. This stance is used effectively before a foot-strike, since the striking leg bears none of the body's weight.

Important points to remember about the cat's-foot stance are the following:

1. The back foot must support the entire weight of the body.

2. The rear foot points at a 45-degree angle away from your opponent. The rear foot is flat on the floor. The toe of the forward foot rests on the floor.

3. The forward toe rests just in front of the rear foot and is pointing at your opponent.

4. Your back and head are straight and facing your opponent.

5. Practice your foot-strikes from this stance without moving the rest of your body. If you move your body before or as you strike, you will telegraph to your opponent the technique you plan to use.

There are other stances used in karate, but those discussed here are the most important. Study them diligently and be able to move into them quickly from any position.

.7

The Karate Thrust

The karate straight thrust or *choku-zuki* was developed
on the principle that the shortest distance between
two points is a straight line. Although there are situations in karate that call for the use of thrusts other
than the straight thrust, your karate training will ben-
efit more if you perfect one thrust rather than half
learn many. Advanced training with the kata will disclose other types of thrusts. Illustrated here are the
Uechi style of karate thrust and the proper karate fist.

■ Important points to remember about the karate
   thrust

   1. When you draw the thrusting arm back to a

*front view, fully
extended thrust*

*complete Uechi thrust with
counter action and withdrawal*

proper karate fist

*view of fully extended
thrust from an angle*

ready-thrust position, the fist is turned palm-up. Inhale as you perform this movement. Remain relaxed.

2. The thrusting fist, when in a ready-thrust position, is drawn back until the fist is parallel with the front of your body.

3. Unless your forearm is extra long, it should be parallel with the floor when in a ready-thrust position. Should your forearm be quite long in proportion to your upper arm, your fist may rest nearer your hip. The ideal position for the thrusting forearm is parallel to the ground.

4. Your fist travels in a straight line when you

THE THRUST **85**

thrust. It twists to a palm-down position while thrusting outward, completing its turn as the arm stops. This twisting movement of the fist adds power to the blow. The shock waves of the thrust will be more penetrating because of the twisting action. Exhale while you thrust. Focus as you complete the thrust.

5. The thrusting arm snaps back to a sanchin arm position (palm-down) immediately after the thrust. If you thrust out with 10 units of power, withdraw the thrust with 20 units of power. Relax your body immediately after focusing. Inhale as you withdraw your thrusting arm. An opponent hit with this whiplike blow (when done correctly) will not fall backward but will fall toward you helpless.

6. Your other arm (counteracting arm) will usually travel to a ready-thrust position as the thrusting arm strikes. (In some kata, the counteracting arm will stay extended. These kata simulate situations where your counteracting arm has a grip on your opponent's arm. In these cases you will pull the person's arm toward you as you thrust. The moving weight of his body toward your thrust will counteract the forward movement of your thrusting arm.)

7. The karate thrust can be delivered from any position along the line formed by the first mentioned thrust. When sparring, you are able to use short thrusts simply by straightening your arm at the elbow and by twisting your fist as described above. Because these thrusts are shorter, they are less powerful than those beginning from a ready-thrust position. They are practical in real situations calling for great speed. Withdraw these thrusts as you did the first, using the breathing and focusing principles developed in the explanation of the thrust and in sanchin.

8. *Keep your fist tightly clenched throughout the thrust.*

9. In practicing this thrust, always thrust out at shoulder height. This is so you can perfect the thrust for the ideal point of contact. In actual situations, however, you will thrust out to the most suited area. Thrusting out at shoulder height develops the muscles of your shoulders, chest, and back evenly and in balance. That is why most of the techniques in karate are performed at 90-degree angles.

10. Practice often in front of a full-length mirror in order to correct mistakes in form.

Concentrate first on developing a thrust that is delivered correctly and smoothly. Then slowly speed up the thrust, keeping the same accurate style. Finally, begin delivering the thrust at full speed. *Do not sacrifice speed for accuracy.*

■ How to develop a fast and effective thrust

Practice the thrust often along with a blocking technique. This will give you practice in changing a defensive technique into an offensive one. Do not hesitate after the block before delivering the thrust. The two movements should be as one. Delay will give your opponent a chance to develop another attack.

Learn to control your thrust. Practice thrusting out at a string or a piece of paper, coming as close to it as possible without hitting it. This practice will be valuable when you spar with another karate-ka whom you do not wish to hit. Later, have someone move his open hand around slowly within thrusting distance. Thrust out at it, using a karate thrust. Attempt to come close to it, but *never* actually hit it. Practice your kicking techniques in this same manner.

Remember that simply repeating a thrust many times will not make you good at karate, just as developing thick calluses on your knuckles will not make you a karate master. You must learn the *correct* way of thrusting. Learn it well, and then work on speed through repetition.

■ Karate thrust exercise

The best way a new student can obtain the speed and accuracy necessary for an effective karate thrust is to practice the thrust in a manner that stresses repetition. The karate thrust exercise shown on the following page is designed to develop these points.

Important points to remember about the thrusting exercise are the following:

1. Remain in a good sanchin stance throughout the exercise.

2. For the first 30 repetitions, remain completely relaxed.

KARATE THRUST EXERCISE

front view of completed thrust, with focus

3. After 30 repetitions, begin to focus the thrust, keeping in mind the following instructions:

a. Remain relaxed as you thrust outward.

b. Tense your body as your fist becomes fully extended.

c. Relax your body immediately after focusing.

d. Withdraw your thrusting arm slightly to prevent it from being rigid and inflexible.

4. Make sure that your fist "corkscrews" out properly. The fist stops twisting when the arm is fully extended. In this position, the fist is facing palm-down, the wrist flat.

5. The elbow of the counteracting arm stops its movement to the rear when the fist of the thrusting arm stops. The counteracting arm retreats with as much power as the thrusting arm.

6. For best results, use the following guide in training:

Week 1: 30 repetitions per workout, all done softly.

Weeks 2, 3, 4: 50 repetitions per workout, all done without strain and without focusing.

(For the first four weeks, the exercise is practiced slowly.)

Weeks 5, 6, 7: 100 repetitions per workout, 50 done slowly and softly, 50 fairly fast and softly.

After 7 weeks: 100 repetitions per workout. Begin to develop the focus. Practice 50 slowly with the focus, then 50 fast with the focus.

■ Summary of the karate thrust

There are two important points to remember about the karate thrust. First, remember that the correct way to thrust is by withdrawing the thrusting arm into a sanchin arm position. Second, remember that, to perfect the thrust, many repetitions of it must be performed, and that practicing the thrust with the full withdrawal is much slower than the thrusting exercise.

There were karate masters in Okinawa who had developed their thrust to such a point of perfection that they were able to break a flowerpot by the shock waves of a thrust. They would thrust at the flowerpot, withdrawing the fist before actually hitting it. The shock waves would shatter the flowerpot. Before a master could perform a feat like this, he would have had to be practicing for at least seven years on the thrusting exercise.

■ Combination blocking and thrusting techniques (uke-zuki-waza)

Illustrated on the following page are a few of the infinite number of possible combination blocking and thrusting techniques available to the karate-ka. Learn the basic ones first. Then develop others, using the kata, the exercises, etc., as guides.

UKE-ZUKI WAZA

blocks (top to bottom):
chudan-soto-uke
gedan-barai
jodan-age-uke
kake-uke

ready-thrust stance

counterattack

∎8

Keri-waza: Foot-striking Techniques

This chapter will discuss the following basic foot-striking techniques: *mae-geri-keage* (front-snap foot-strike), *mae-geri-kekomi* (front foot-thrust), *yoko-geri-kekomi* (side foot-thrust), *mae-tobi-geri* (flying front foot-strike), and others.

■ Basic principles of sanchin used in foot-striking and foot-thrusting techniques

1. Proper focus.

The striking leg remains relaxed until the moment of contact. This will allow you to get maximum speed from the foot-strike. As the foot reaches its objective, tense all the muscles in your body. This will transmit the power of your body into the foot-strike.

2. Co-ordination.

Make all movements smooth and precise. Jerky or unsure movements sap much of the power and speed that could be applied to the technique.

3. Stability.

Never lift the heel of your supporting foot off the floor. A stable stance is necessary for maximum power.

■ Mae-geri-keage (front-snap foot-strike)

The important points to remember about the front-snap foot-strike are as follows:

a. *basic hachiji-dachi stance*
b. *initial step-in (to front) or step-out (to rear)*
c. *knee in cocked position, striking foot in close*
d. *strike to a straight position*
e. *withdraw striking foot to cocked position*
f. *recover striking foot to left or right sanchin stance by stepping either in or out*

attack, block, and counterattack

1. Be in a firm and stable position before attempting the foot-strike. After stepping in or out (forward or to the rear), raise the knee of the striking leg as high as possible while keeping the striking foot in a cocked position close to the body. When the knee is at its highest, the foot begins its forward and upward movement.

2. Keep your back and head straight. Do not bend forward as you strike. Bending forward indicates a strain caused by tight leg muscles. Work harder on the correct exercises that will help this problem. (See final paragraph of this chapter.)

3. At the highest point of your strike, the legs should be straight. Your back and head should be straight also.

4. After the point of impact, withdraw the foot quickly to a position close to your body. This prevents your opponent from grabbing the leg.

5. Return the striking leg quickly to a stable sanchin stance, either to the front or to the rear.

HOW NOT TO FOOT-STRIKE

It is essential to insert a word of caution about the faulty foot-strike. It is obvious from the picture why the foot-strike is ineffective. Besides being off balance, the striker has weakened his ability to kick by allowing the heel of the supporting leg to leave the floor.

how not to foot-strike

a. *basic hachiji-dachi stance*
b. *step-in (to front) or step-out (to rear)*
c. *knee in cocked position, striking foot in close*
d. *thrust: foot travels in straight line; knee pushes downward until leg is straight*
e. *withdraw thrusting foot to cocked position*
f. *recover to left or right sanchin stance*

■ Mae-geri-kekomi (front foot-thrust)

This foot-thrust can be applied by using either the ball of the foot or the heel. The ball of the foot is used to strike softer sections of the body, such as the stomach, etc. The heel is used for striking the harder parts, such as the solar plexus, knees, etc. Important points to remember about mae-geri-kekomi are as follows:

1. In the cocked position shown in *c,* be sure that the knee of your thrusting foot is close to your body

APPLICATION

block with foot-thrust

f

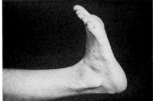

heel of foot thrust

and as high as possible. The higher the knee is, the more power your thrust will have.

2. Keep your head and back straight throughout the technique.

3. When your thrusting leg is fully extended, it should be straight and parallel with the floor.

4. Withdraw the thrusting leg quickly to the front or rear sanchin position.

5. Refer to points 1 and 4 under mae-geri-keage.

WHEN TO USE MAE-GERI-KEAGE AND MAE-GERI-KEKOMI

These techniques may be used to strike an opponent's chin, neck, armpit, stomach, or groin. The strikes are the most effective if your opponent does not realize that you are able to use your feet. Use the element of surprise whenever possible. When faced with an opponent who is using a knife, keep out of his reach without using your feet. Your opponent will not suspect that you can use your feet and therefore will be less careful. When you see an opportunity, step forward enough so that your striking foot will reach his mid-section but his knife will not reach you. Deliver a fast mae-geri-keage or mae-geri-kekomi.

YOKO-GERI-KEAGE *(chudan area)*

■ Yoko-geri-keage (side-snap foot-strike)

This foot-strike may be used effectively when you are attacked from the side. You are able to defend either of your sides without giving up or weakening your front position. Strike directly to your left or right flank for the exercise. This foot-strike is practiced at two heights: *chudan* (middle area) and *gedan* (low area), as shown here. Important points to remember about yoko-geri-keage are the following:

1. Raise the striking leg until your knee is in line with your belt. Your striking foot is placed next to your other knee. The knife edge of your striking foot is pointing toward your opponent.

2. The supporting leg is bent outward at the knee for stability.

3. Your back and head remain straight throughout the technique, although in actual use there are times when a "lean-out" is desirable, as against a knife, etc.

4. The striking leg is straight at the point of impact.

5. Remember to withdraw the striking leg to a "cocked" position immediately. Then return it to a hachiji-dachi or sanchin stance.

WHEN TO USE YOKO-GERI-KEAGE

The best time to use this foot-strike is when you are attacked from the side. Use the surprise element by not turning toward the opponent but rather by striking with the yoko-geri-keage. You can also be facing an opponent and actually turn away from him. As you turn away, strike out with the foot-strike. Remember that your leg is longer than his arm and that this will give you an advantage over him.

chudan area

APPLICATION

gedan area

chudan foot-thrust (middle area)

gedan foot-thrust (low area)

■ **Yoko-geri-kekomi** (side foot-thrust)

Like yoko-geri-keage, this technique is performed at the two levels of chudan and gedan. Important points to remember about yoko-geri-kekomi are the following:

1. In the ready-thrust leg position, the knee of your thrusting leg will point at your opponent. The thrusting foot is resting against the knee of the supporting leg. The side of the thrusting foot is pointing at your opponent.

2. In the thrust, push out with your foot and down with your knee until the leg is straight. The outside of the thrusting foot is bent out so that the knife edge of your foot is the striking surface.

3. The supporting leg must always be in a stable position. The knee acts as a stabilizer by being bent

out slightly. Your foot is always flat on the floor. *Never* rise up on your toes.

4. Keep your back and head straight in this technique except when defending yourself against a knife. Against a knife, you will find that leaning out—away from the knife—is advisable.

5. After the thrust, withdraw the thrusting foot back to a ready-thrust (cocked) position immediately. Then return to a good sanchin position.

WHEN TO USE YOKO-GERI-KEKOMI

The best time to use this technique is after blocking an arm thrust. Pull the opponent toward you, using his body momentum as you execute a yoko-geri-kekomi to his knee.

defense against a front attack

defense against a rear attack

■ Ushiro-geri-kekomi (back foot-thrust)

The technique of ushiro-geri-kekomi—the back foot-thrust—is employed as a defense against both front and rear attack. The points to be remembered about the technique are as follows:

1. Front attack.

a. If at all possible, stay at least two arm-lengths away from your opponent if he has a knife. Take a step forward, enough so that you can reach him with your leg but so that he cannot reach you with his knife. Raise your thrusting leg so that your knee is high and your thrusting foot is close to your body, with your toes pointing toward your opponent. Twist your body around so that your chest is parallel with the floor. Thrust out quickly with your thrusting leg and withdraw it immediately to a ready-thrust position. This whole technique is executed in one movement.

b. Twist your head to the side as you attack, so that you are able to see your opponent at all times.

THE WAY OF KARATE 100

c. Bend the supporting leg slightly for a stability.

d. Your body and leg should be straight and parallel to the floor at the point of contact.

e. After completing the thrust, twist your body around until you again face your opponent, returning the thrusting foot to a forward or rear sanchin position.

2. Rear attack.

a. Look at your opponent by turning your head. Lean forward as you raise your thrusting leg into a ready-thrust postition.

b. The thrust and withdrawal are the same as they were in the front attack.

WHEN TO USE USHIRO-GERI-KEKOMI

The best time to use ushiro-geri-kekomi is when you are being attacked from the front by an opponent who has a knife. You have the advantage of reach and surprise. Because the leg thrusts out in a straight line, it is extremely hard to block. I use a knife as an example because it is one of the most dangerous weapons commonly used.

APPLICATIONS

from a standing start

from a crouched stance

■ Mae-tobi-geri (flying front foot-strike)

This technique (shown above) is begun from either a standing position or a crouched stance. Important points to remember about it are the following:

1. Best results from this strike are obtained if you take at least one step forward before jumping. This distance gives you the necessary momentum needed for a well-executed strike.

2. The take-off (with left leg):

a. Step on the left leg. As you do, bend the left knee slightly. Spring into the air about three feet. Bring your right leg up to a cocked position as you leave the floor.

b. Keep your back straight throughout the technique.

3. Land in a good sanchin stance with your arms in a sparring position, ready for another technique.

4. Do not jump for distance but mainly for height. When you reach the apex of the jump, strike out to your opponent's stomach with your right foot. Your opponent's guard will drop when your foot strikes. Use this opportunity to strike his neck, chin, or face with your left foot.

5. The mae-tobi-geri from a crouched stance: This technique can be used as a defense against an attack from the front or the rear. If attacked from the rear, fall forward, keeping your left foot in place, and turn toward your attacker. Your weight should be on your right leg, as shown in the pictures. Spring to a standing position by pushing upward with your right leg. Continue the movement into the air by pushing up with your left leg. The technique continues as in the ordinary mae-tobi-geri.

6. The mae-tobi-geri from a crouched stance can be used when you are attacked from the front:

APPLICATION

a. Fall back on your bent right leg. Keep your left foot in place and your left leg straight. Throughout this technique your body continues to face your opponent.

b. In the ready-jump position your arms are straight and pointing in the direction of your opponent. When you jump, your arms go into a sparring position.

■ General remarks on keri-waza

This completes the basic foot-strikes and foot-thrusts you must learn. Once you have mastered these, you can use the same techniques with slight variations. Remember that you must try to perfect every movement in order to become really good at karate. Half-learned movements are as good as no movements.

When you are able to do a foot technique without referring to the book, I suggest that you then learn the term for the technique by repeating its name aloud while executing it. Later, when you have learned all of the names, have someone call out any technique at random and then follow through with the technique called for.

Should you have any difficulties with the keri-waza, check the following points to see if your trouble is caused by posture difficulties. Correct the problem by working on the correcting exercise.

TROUBLE	CORRECTIVE EXERCISE
Cannot keep back straight.	Hip, thigh, and back exercises shown in Chapter 3: waist "scoop," trunk-stretching exercise, straight-leg striking exercise, side-stretching exercise, and front leg-stretching exercise.
Cannot keep balance.	Work with sanchin and with exercises shown in Chapter 3: trunk-stretching exercise and leg lift and turn exercise.
Trouble with foot techniques.	Hip, thigh, and back exercises listed above.

attack to head blocked by jodan-age-uke

∎ 9

Uke-waza: Blocking Techniques

This chapter describes and explains the basic blocks which you should learn first. As you progress, study the kata, the kumite, and the exercises for advanced blocking techniques. When studying a new technique, break it down into three or more parts. Study the basic arm movements first. Then work on the foot movements. Finally, combine the two movements into one, keeping in mind the various points that you should remember. The following is an outline of the blocks presented in this chapter:

chudan-uke, middle-area block
> *chudan-uchi-uke,* inside (50%) middle-area block
> *chudan-soto-uke,* outside (75%) middle-area block

gedan-barai, downward block
> (from a sanchin stance)
> (from a low stance)

jodan-age-uke, upper rising block

■ Explanation of terminology

1. Chudan-uchi-uke: Chudan-uke is the term used to represent karate blocks that protect the middle area of the body. Uchi means that the block is performed to the inside of the attacker's defense. The blocker's counterattack, if performed with the attacker's second attempt at an attack, has a 50% chance of success.

2. Chudan-soto-uke: Soto means that this block is performed so that, at the completion of the block, the defense of the attacking man is to the outside. The counterattack has a 75% chance of being successful because of the superior position.

The remaining blocks are explained at length with their descriptions below.

■ Circular defense principles

The chudan-uke uses the principle of circular defense to block a thrust. By this, I mean that the blocks do not depend entirely on brute force to block a thrust, but instead they employ a circular path that reaches out, neutralizes, and finally changes the direction of the thrust. The diagram on the following page explains this principle. Note how the blocking arm changes the direction of the thrusting arm gradually, shifting the opponent's balance until he loses his center of gravity. As your opponent attempts to regain his balance, your counterattack, even though not as powerful as his attack, will be very effective.

In the diagram, block A is a block delivered at a 90-degree angle. Note that more power is required to change the direction of the thrust. Block B (the path used in the chudan-uke) reaches out in a circular

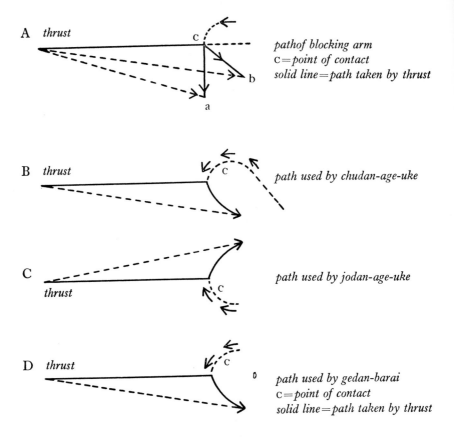

A *thrust*

pathof blocking arm
c=*point of contact*
solid line=path taken by thrust

B *thrust*

path used by chudan-age-uke

C
thrust

path used by jodan-age-uke

D *thrust*

path used by gedan-barai
c=*point of contact*
solid line=path taken by thrust

movement, meets the attacking force, and shifts the attack to a harmless direction. The circular block does not attempt to stop the blow; in fact, the momentum of your opponent's forward movement is finally changed to your advantage.

The diagram above illustrates the paths used in the chudan-uke, the jodan-age-uke, and the gedan-barai.

After changing the direction of the thrust, pull your opponent forward as you counterattack. The forward momentum of your opponent, plus the striking power of your counterattack, will make your counterattack twice as effective. Through the use of this principle, you can meet and overcome with a small amount of force a much greater attacking force.

■ Chudan-uchi-uke (inside middle-area block)

This basic crane block, illustrated on the following two pages is designed to deflect a one-two thrust combination. Even though at first this block does not appear to be as effective as others shown, it is the most important block in karate. Once you have mastered this block, you can use an infinite number of variations from it without having to study them individually. The variations will come naturally as you study the basic block. It is impossible to show in a book every defense that there is against every type of offense. Even if you were actually studying under a karate master, you would not practice all of the variations of the basic blocks.

You would, instead, learn and practice the basic blocks and kata. Once these were mastered, you would be able to defend yourself in nearly any situation. I mention this now simply to let you know that you need not actually spar with an opponent in order to develop defensive reflexes. Later in your karate training, sparring will prove valuable simply to give you confidence and the feel of actual combat. The old masters in Okinawa never had their students spar because they believed that if a student practiced his kata enough he would naturally develop the feel of the techniques he was studying and would be able to use them when the need arose.

IMPORTANT POINTS TO REMEMBER ABOUT CHUDAN-UCHI-UKE

1. Start off in a good hachiji-dachi stance. From this position you should be prepared to move into any stance and perform any technique.

2. Make sure your elbows are in line with your body when you start the technique, and be sure they are in the same position when the movement stops. Your elbows should only move straight up or down in this block.

3. The forearm of your arm that makes the first block travels in a circular outward movement. Do not grab the thrusting arm. You may be able to block slow-moving thrusts in this manner, but the fast ones will surely get by. For this reason, avoid practicing this block with a partner until you have perfected it.

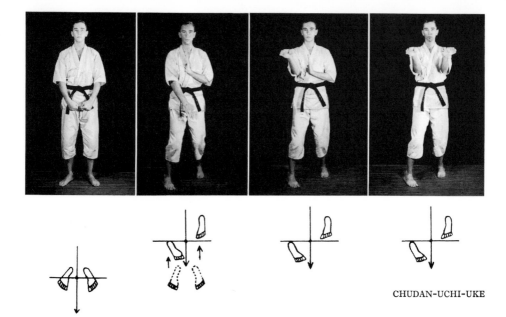

CHUDAN-UCHI-UKE

You will not then be tempted to block incorrectly when you block a simulated thrust.

4. Keep the hand of your blocking arm even with your forearm. As the blocking hand reaches the thrusting arm, it bends to the side slightly to hook the thrusting arm. The wrist is still straight. The finger tips are bent down, and the thumb is tucked in.

5. The blocking arm travels in a circular path, the finger tips never going above eye level.

6. Practice this block by the numbers:

a. Right arm blocks first. Place left arm on chest, the left hand protecting your solar plexus.

b. Circular block with right arm, stopping in a sanchin arm position.

c. Block outward with left arm, stopping in a sanchin arm position.

7. Practice this block slowly by the numbers at first, gradually picking up speed until the two blocks are performed without hesitation. Do not sacrifice precision of form for speed. Speed will come only after the movement is a reflex action. If you attempt to speed up a movement before that time, you will find yourself developing poor and dangerous reflexes.

8. After the arm movements come easy to you, start developing the ability to step to the rear into a good sanchin foot stance as you perform the block. Your arm and foot movements should begin together and end together. When you complete the block, you have to be in a good solid position in order to counterattack effectively.

HOW AND WHEN TO USE CHUDAN-UCHI-UKE

The basic chudan-uchi-uke is ideally suited for an inside attack. Example: A man attacks you from the front with a left thrust to the face and follows through with a right to the heart. You usually do not know how the man is going to follow through with an attack. After deflecting his left thrust with your right arm, you are prepared to deflect his right arm if necessary, or you could counterattack with a shuto-uchi (knife-hand strike) to his neck.

Step to the rear with your left foot into a sanchin stance as you deflect the thrust with your right forearm. Keep your arm in that position, holding the man's forearm. Block the right thrust with your left forearm if necessary. This block is effective because you end up with both of the man's arms in your grip. Use his forward momentum to pull him toward you as you deliver a knee to his face.

This is a very simple example. Once you have deflected the thrusts, you can perform any number of excellent techniques.

APPLICATION

CHUDAN-SOTO-UKE *(with sliding step to rear)* ←

■ Chudan-soto-uke (outside middle-area block)

This ready-thrust block is derived, as are all the middle-area blocks, from the basic crane block. The difference is that in this block you deflect the thrusting arm to the outside and end up in a ready-thrust position with your counteracting arm. In this position you are able to counterattack quickly. Sidestep to the rear and to the side as you perform the block. By sidestepping, you guide rather than push your opponent's arm away. This sidestep to the rear, combined with a circular block, enables a small person to block a powerful man's thrust.

IMPORTANT POINTS TO REMEMBER ABOUT CHUDAN-SOTO-UKE

1. Start off in a good hachiji-dachi position.
2. Practice the block alone before combining it with the foot movements.
3. As the blocking arm moves, the counteracting arm moves into a ready-thrust position. The two movements should coincide. The counteracting arm travels up from the hachiji-dachi position until it reaches the elbow of the blocking arm. It then moves into the ready-thrust position. The upward movement counterbalances the movement of the blocking arm and speeds it up.
4. Sidestep to the right rear to block an opponent's

foot movements used in chudan-soto-uke

left arm-thrust, to the left to block his right arm-thrust.

5. The sidestep to the rear counteracts any forward movement of your opponent. You regulate the size of your step by the size of your opponent's step. You move your foot back on the side that your opponent is thrusting from. Follow through with your other foot into a forward sanchin position. (Forward because it is the last foot to move, and it is placed in the forward position.)

6. Keep your back and head straight throughout this block.

7. Do not bob up and down while you sidestep, but keep your eyes on the same level throughout the block. *Watch your opponent's eyes.*

HOW TO USE CHUDAN-SOTO-UKE

I can best explain how to use this block by giving you an example and explaining how to apply it. A man attacks you with a hard left thrust to the chin. You sidestep to the right, blocking his arm safely away from your body with your left forearm. When you complete the block, your forearm slides down his arm, and your hand grips his wrist. Keep your elbow close to your side and pull the man toward you. At the same time, counterattack with a foot-thrust.

APPLICATION

KAKE-UKE *(with sliding step to rear)* ←

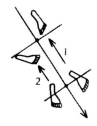

*foot movements used
in kake-uke*

APPLICATION

■ Kake-uke (inside hooking block)

This inside hooking block is used mainly as a defense against surprise attacks. Because the block is fast, it can block a thrust that would ordinarily have taken you by surprise. The kake-uke allows you to deflect a thrust quickly without sidestepping. You must be quick in your counterattack, however, because your opponent's other arm is still free and able to follow through with another attack. You may, if you have time, sidestep and use the kake-uke as an outside block.

IMPORTANT POINTS TO REMEMBER ABOUT KAKE-UKE

1. The blocking arm moves in a circular path and stops in a sanchin arm position.

2. If you block with your right arm, step back with your left foot into a sanchin stance. Your foot stops when your arm stops.

3. Keep your back and head straight.

4. Do not move your shoulders in this block— only your arms.

5. The counteracting arm moves into a ready-thrust position in the same way as in the ready-thrust block.

6. Counterattack immediately with a foot-strike or thrust.

APPLICATION
(against a low thrust)

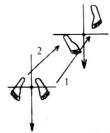

foot movements used in gedan-barai: left foot (1) moves to left rear first, followed by right foot (2)

■ **Gedan-barai** (downward block)

This downward block is used mainly for blocking foot-strikes, but it can be used effectively for low thrusts also. When used as a defense against a foot-strike, keep your fist clenched. Your deflecting power will be increased if you do. When blocking a low thrust, keep your hand open and straight. Speed is most important in blocking a thrust, and your block will be faster if you block with an open hand. Your thrusting arm counteracts into a ready-thrust position.

IMPORTANT POINTS TO REMEMBER ABOUT GEDAN-BARAI

1. Begin your practice of the gedan-barai by standing in the hachiji-dachi stance and repeating the block until it is done correctly.

2. When you are in the ready-block position, as shown in *c,* your arm is close to your body. Your fist is closed and touching your neck.

3. On the downward swing, your fist twists into the striking leg so that the edge of your forearm strikes. While practicing, continue the downward movement until the arm is straight.

4. As the blocking arm travels downward, the counteracting arm moves into a ready-thrust position. The two movements begin and end together.

5. When you have learned the arm movement well,

APPLICATION *(against a knife attack)*

develop the sidestep to the rear with the block. Should your opponent thrust low with his right arm or kick with his right leg, step to the left and block with your right arm.

6. Keep your head and back straight throughout this block.

WHEN AND HOW TO USE GEDAN-BARAI

Keep at least two arm lengths defended at all times. When your opponent lunges forward with a foot-strike, step lightly to the side, deflecting the foot-strike and counterattacking with a foot-strike or thrust.

■ **Gedan-barai, low stance**

This variation of the gedan-barai (opposite page) is performed with a low stance. The block can be used for thrusts of all kinds, since the circular path of the block effectively protects your whole body. Because the block is strong, it can be used against foot-strikes.

IMPORTANT POINTS TO REMEMBER ABOUT GEDAN-BARAI, LOW STANCE

1. Practice the footwork of this block first:

a. Take a large step forward or to the rear with your right foot. When your foot touches the floor, continue the downward movement of your body until you are in the low stance.

b. In this stance, remember to keep your back and head straight.

c. Push yourself back to a sanchin stance with your right foot, the right foot remaining to the front.

APPLICATION *(low stance)*

2. Next, practice the arm movements alone:

a. Keep your left arm extended while performing a block with your right arm. Your right arm blocks in a counterclockwise circular pattern in front of your face. As your right arm descends from the circular block, your left arm counteracts into a ready-thrust position while your right arm continues downward. The right arm stops when it is in line with your right leg.

b. Make sure the arms move together and stop together.

3. Combine the two movements:

a. As you take a step forward or to the rear, your arm performs the block. When your body stops in the low stance, your arms should complete the block.

b. With your right foot, push yourself back into a sanchin stance. Your arms return to a ready position.

JODAN-AGE-UKE *(with closed fist for maximum power)*

■ **Jodan-age-uke (upper rising block)**

This upper rising block can be performed in two ways: from a sanchin stance and from a low stance. You can increase the power of your block by grasping the blocking arm with your other hand and by pushing upward with both arms (opposite page).

IMPORTANT POINTS TO REMEMBER ABOUT JODAN-AGE-UKE

1. From a sanchin stance.

a. Start the block by bringing your right arm to a ready-thrust position. Keep your left arm extended.

b. From the ready-thrust position, push up and to the left with your right arm. Counteract the blocking movement by bringing your left arm to a ready-thrust position.

c. When your right fist reaches chest level, it begins to turn from a palm-upward position to a position

APPLICATION *(with open hand for maximum speed)*

JODAN-AGE-UKE *(from low stance)*

where it faces your opponent. The edge of your forearm is up.

d. Continue the upward movement until your forearm is at a 45-degree angle.

2. From a low stance.

a. The same arm movements are used as in the above.

b. Either a forward or a rearward step is used with the above arm block. The same low stance is used in this blocking technique as was used in gedan-barai.

c. Co-ordinate the arm and leg movements so that they begin and end together.

how to increase power of jodan-age-uke

■ Uke-keri-waza: combinations of blocking and foot-
striking techniques

Practice various combinations of blocks and foot-strikes (next page) to develop co-ordination and speed. The combinations should be smooth and should follow through effortlessly.

COMBINED BLOCKING AND FOOT-STRIKING TECHNIQUES

*ready-attack
position*

attack with block

*foot-thrusting and foot-
striking counterattack*

■ 10

Other Karate Exercises and Techniques

It is the purpose of this chapter to introduce another group of important karate exercises and techniques. These will be discussed under the headings of *kake* (co-ordinating and stabilizing exercise), arm-strengthening exercise, *yakusoku-kumite* (advanced prearranged sparring exercise), turning techniques, and technique combinations.

■ Kake (co-ordinating and stabilizing exercise)

The purpose of this exercise (see next page) is to develop co-ordination and stability. It should be done at every workout before the arm-strengthening exercise. The sequence of movements should be repeated about 15 times. Then change the foot stance and repeat the movements with your other arm.

IMPORTANT POINTS TO REMEMBER ABOUT KAKE

1. In the ready position, your left arm is in a san-chin position, fist closed and palm turned up. Your right arm remains in a ready-thrust position throughout the exercise.

2. The first movement is a slow upward thrust with the left arm. As the arm rises, the left hand opens (the right hand remains in a fist) and turns clockwise until it has turned 180 degrees. The palm is turned down at the completion of the upward thrust.

3. The purpose of the exercise is to massage the forearm, stimulating circulation. When done correctly, the exercise develops a sense of balance and stability that is useful in all of your karate techniques. This stability is acquired by a slow, forceful upward thrust

KAKE. *The foot chart shows how to get into kake position.*

that is performed in such a way that the performer will not fall off balance if his partner should suddenly let up the pressure on his arm. This test of stability should be made several times during the exercise.

4. When the arm is fully extended upward, you will be ready to perform the second phase of the exercise: the downward pull into a sanchin arm position. As the arm is lowered, the hand turns until it is again facing palm upward.

5. The upward thrust represents a karate thrust. The upward movement against the power of your partner's arm strengthens your arm. Because the power of your partner's arm is changeable, you develop a sense of balance and stability.

6. The downward pull in this exercise represents a karate block. Again, the power of your partner's arm against yours strengthens your blocking power.

7. When the second phase of this exercise is completed, your or your partner's stability can again be tested by grabbing his wrist with your blocking arm and pulling in. If his stability is weak, he will easily be pulled off balance. Test your partner at least twice during this exercise.

thrusts. The main purpose of
tion the arms so that they can
all attacks. The secondary p
of karate reflex actions.

After you have learned th
go through it *correctly* with
book, then start practicing
of Zen described in the ch

Whenever possible, have
exercise and make corre
learning, stop after each m
tions yourself.

■ Arm-strengthening exercise

The main purpose of this exercise (see following two pages) is to strengthen the forearm and wrist. The exercise also gives the new student his first opportunity to use his blocking techniques with a partner. Repeat the sequence as shown about a dozen times. Then begin the exercise again, this time reversing the action and using your right arm instead of the left. The attacker steps forward with his right leg. The defender steps to the rear with his right leg.

IMPORTANT POINTS TO REMEMBER ABOUT THE ARM-STRENGTHENING EXERCISE

1. Remember to thrust and block in the correct karate style.

2. When you first learn the exercise, practice it slowly and easily or your arms will become very sore. You must develop strength in the forearm slowly and increase the power of the strikes very little every week.

3. When striking, do not hit the same spot every time but distribute the strikes all over your partner's forearm.

4. Your arm movements and foot movements should correspond. When you thrust with your right arm, your right leg should complete its movement as the arm completes its thrust. The same holds true for the When you block with your left arm, the right leg should blocks. complete its step to the rear when the block is completed.

5. The second block is a variation of the kake-uke, so study it carefully.

6. Keep your back and shoulders facing straig
forward as you do this exercise. Never throw yc
shoulder for ward when you thrust.

7. When you complete the thrust, your arm st
relaxed and straight while your partner blocks for
second time.

8. Focus your arm muscles as your partner stril

9. After completing this exercise, massage the a
muscles for a minute to relax them.

SUMMARY OF THE ARM-STRENGTHENING EXERCIS

Practice this exercise using only the movem
shown in the illustrations. Never use other block

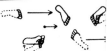

■ Yakusoku-kumite (advanced prearranged sparring exercise)

The purpose of this exercise is to develop defensive and counterattacking techniques in the student under realistic conditions. Many techniques and technique combinations are used. Some of the blocks are variations of the basic blocks already described. Study these carefully.

Repeat this exercise about 10 times per training schedule while learning it. Bow in the proper manner before and after the kumite. As part of the Oriental karate outlook, the person who attacks first loses the kumite.

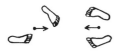

attacker (A):
ready thrust position
defender (D):
informal stance

A : right-arm thrust,
double sliding step forward
D : double sliding step to
left rear, right outside block

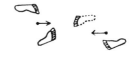

D : ready foot strike position

D : right foot strike

A : left thrust, step forward
D : step back to right rear,
left outside block

D : left snap foot-strike

D : right-arm thrust,
   step forward
A : step back to left rear,
   right outside block and
   right snap foot strike

D : left-arm thrust,
   double sliding step forward
A : step back to right rear,
   lefoutsidet block

A : left snap foot strike

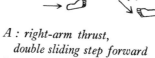

A : left snap foot strike,
   withdraw leg to
   left sanchin position

A : right-arm thrust,
   double sliding step forward
D : double sliding step to left
   rear, right outside block

D : left spear-hand
   thrust

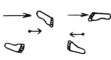

A : left-arm thrust,
   step forward
D : step back,
   right palm-heel block

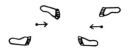

D : left fore-knuckle strike,
   right arm returns to
   ready thrust pasition

D : right-arm thrust,
   step forward
A : step to the rear,
   right forearm inside block

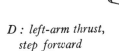

D : left-arm thrust,
   step forward
A : step back,
   right inside forearm block

A : double forearm block
D : left-arm thrust

A : right back-fist strike

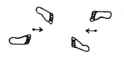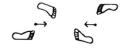

A : arm withdrawn

A : ready thrust position
D : arms lowered to
defence position

A : right-arm thrust,
step forward
D : step back, left inside
middle-area block

A : left-arm thrust,
step forward
D : step back,
right inside middle-area block

D : upward knee kick

WALKING OR RUNNING TURN

■ Karate turning techniques

Besides the basic sanchin turn, there is one other turn that is used while walking or running. The most important point to remember about both of these turns, when used in a defensive technique, is that you must be prepared to deflect the attacking blow immediately. The main principles behind these turns are stability, speed, and alertness. The stability comes from having one foot firmly on the ground throughout the turn. Speed comes through practice. The alertness is developed from the karate-Zen training.

IMPORTANT POINTS TO REMEMBER ABOUT THE TURN-ING TECHNIQUES

1. Whenever you turn, know what is happening behind you before the turn is completed. This is done by turning your head to the rear as you turn.

2. Even before you complete the turn, begin the blocking technique necessary to deflect the thrust or foot-strike.

3. Always keep your body in a good sanchin stance. Do not lean forward or to the rear. The slightly bent knees act as stabilizers. Do not straighten them while executing the turn.

4. Co-ordinate the turn with any defensive technique that you may use. When your feet stop, the

blocking technique should have been completed, and you should be ready to counterattack.

5. Complete the turn by going into a sanchin stance. This will give you maximum all-around stability.

6. When someone grabs you by the shoulder and pulls you around with the intention of hitting you, use the sanchin turn, deflecting the arm on your shoulder with your arm and at the same time beginning a chudan-soto-uke with your other arm. If the person grabs your left shoulder, use your left arm to deflect his arm. When you complete the turn, you should be in a sanchin arm position, ready to counterattack. You could counterattack by pulling his arms in and down and by using your right knee to strike him in the groin, chest, or face. (See next technique.)

■ **Application of the running turn**

At start of attack, step forward with left leg. Look to rear. Step around with the left leg and deflect the attack. Bring the right leg around into a sanchin stance. Pull your opponent inward, using his forward momentum. Then counterattack with a left foot-strike.

■ Basic turning block

At the beginning of the attack, when someone grabs you by the shoulder, attempting to turn you around, place your hand on his. Then execute a sanchin turn, deflecting the arm on your shoulder with an inside block. Place your right hand on your solar plexus to deflect another attack. Complete the crane block. Pull your opponent toward you as you execute a foot-strike.

■ Technique combinations

Practicing the combinations shown on the following pages will help you acquire the ability to change stances and techniques quickly without weakening your position. The combinations discussed are mae-geri-keage and choku-zuki (front-snap foot-strike and thrust); chudan-soto-uke and yoko-geri-kekomi (outside middle area block and side foot-thrust); fishtail block and thrust; and double thrusting technique.

■ Mae-geri-keage and choku-zuki

Assume the ready-attack stance. Step forward and begin with a right foot-strike. After the completed foot-strike, withdraw the striking leg. Step forward and thrust with the right arm. The thrust is co-ordinated with the forward step. When the step is completed, the thrust is also completed. Withdraw the thrusting arm to a sanchin position, fist facing downward.

■ Chudan-soto-uke and yoko-geri-kekomi

Step to the rear as you execute a right outside block. Co-ordinate the block with the step. After the completed step and block, assume the ready-thrust foot stance. Complete the foot-thrust to a simulated opponent's knee. Then go into the withdrawal stance.

outside

inside

■ Fishtail block and thrust

Besides being an excellent exercise for the wrists, this technique develops three very effective blocks: *teisho-uke* (inside wrist-block), *kakuto-uke* (outside wrist-block), and *tsuki-uke* (thrusting block).

The beginning stance calls for a sanchin arm position with hand vertical. In the outside wrist-block the arm moves parallel to the floor. The fingers always trail during this technique. For the inside wrist-block, the finger tips remain still while the wrist moves from right to the left position until the hand is bent properly. This sequence should be repeated about 15 times.

After completing this series of movements, bring

THRUSTING BLOCK

your arm to a sanchin position, fist upward. In the thrusting block keep your elbow bent outward for the thrust. Your forearm will block a thrust as your fist makes contact. Withdraw your arm to a sanchin position, fist down.

The application of the fishtail block calls first for an outside wrist-block and then for a counterattack using a back-fist strike.

■ Double thrusting technique

This technique can be used for counterattacking or for blocking. To use it for blocking, turn the hands

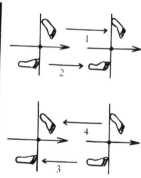

over and bend the elbow outward as you strike (similar to a thrusting block). This technique is used primarily for developing co-ordination and balance.

Assume the ready-thrust stance. Step forward with a sliding step and at the completion of the step thrust outward with both arms. (See foot chart, which shows how feet move from position *a* to position *b*. In the withdrawal, the arms return to a sanchin position.

To continue the exercise, make a sliding step to the rear. At the completion of the step, thrust outward. In the foot chart showing the second part of the exercise, the right foot moves first.

▪ 11

Advanced Kata: Seisan

To explain the significance of the kata, their meanings, and their purposes is very difficult. In first studying karate the kata resemble a dance or, at the most, a separate part of karate. The meaning or interpretation of the kata can never be explained satisfactorily with words. It must be felt intuitively by the student. This method of teaching corresponds to the method used by the Buddhist monks. The monks did not attempt to "word-feed" Buddhism to their followers but set up conditions in which their students would experience within themselves the ideal state of mind they were striving for.

In both karate and Zen Buddhism the experience of the mind-body relationship that is the foundation for both ways of life must be arrived at through the student's application of principles founded by the masters. In Zen Buddhism these principles are many, and they vary according to the master. In karate, these principles are the kata. Different styles of karate have different kata. These kata must, in order to be termed kata, perform the function of setting up conditions within the student conducive to his arriving at the necessary state of mind. This state of mind is widely accepted by all true karate schools. It is the ability to perform all actions, both in karate and in life, with the mind-body relationship developed initially in Zen and in sanchin. Only schools having sanchin or a comparable Zen exercise can accomplish this.

What purpose, then, do the advanced kata have if sanchin performs all the necessary functions of the kata? In order to answer this question, we must first analyze again, as a whole, the purpose of the kata. The first question that must be answered is "Why do we have so many kata?" There are over fifty recognized kata in the four styles making up the Okinawan Karate Association. Each kata was designed and developed with certain points or techniques in mind obscure in other kata. Each one performed a little better what was in an older kata but executed with less function.

In the analysis of the kata, I will speak only from the experience that I have had in studying the Uechi-ryu karate (formerly pangai-noon in China). There seems to be a pattern that makes sense in the arrangement and formulation of the three main kata in this style. Although many other kata are taught, they perform only one function, which is that of helping the student to understand the more complex basic three.

The kata form a complete circle: the beginning is the end, and the end is the beginning. The student begins his training with sanchin, and he ends his training with sanchin. To better understand this circle, we must try to understand all three kata—not the meanings (this takes many years) but the basic movements. By understanding the basic movements, we can gain insight to the meaning of the circle.

First, sanchin is composed of seemingly simple movements that are readily understood by a new student. You should by now be familiar with the basic movements. Do you see anything hidden in these movements? Sanchin readily discloses to the new student the methods of stepping, thrusting, and breathing. There is nothing particularly amazing or unusual about this. Without being told, the student accepts sanchin at face value and learns the movements, completely unaware of their significance. After a period of many months, the master begins to teach the student seisan (pronounced "say-sahn"). In this kata the apparent techniques are more numerous and more visible. The student believes that, because many techniques are easy to recognize, as soon as he knows the kata by memory he has mastered it.

After studying both sanchin and seisan for a number of years, the student begins to develop the apparent techniques of seisan into reflexes. This progress is apparent within the student. He recognizes his progress and feels that he knows everything there is to be known about karate.

After still more training with both kata, the student becomes aware that techniques which are apparent, or easily seen, in seisan were present in sanchin. These hidden, or not apparent, techniques in sanchin have been completely concealed from him up to this time. This starts him to thinking. If so much was present but hidden from him in a simple kata like sanchin, then how many techniques are hidden in seisan? At this point the student reaches the stage that the Zen student reaches when the master gives him a *koan,* or seemingly senseless riddle, to solve. Both students realize that the answer is within the riddle, but neither knows how or where to start solving it.

About this time, the master will teach the student san-ju-roku. In this kata, many of the hidden movements of seisan are shown openly. This the new student does not recognize immediately, for he has not thought that these movements existed up to now.

After many years of training with all three kata, the student begins to see new meanings in the movements of seisan. Through the study of san-ju-roku, he finds that seisan contains the very same movements, only in a more subtle form. In a still more subtle form he finds these same techniques in sanchin.

You are probably asking yourself at this point: Why the intermediate steps of sanchin and seisan? Why not teach the student san-ju-roku right away and be done with it?

The answer to this question could become extremely complex, covering subjects as seemingly unrelated as philosophy and body dynamics. The purpose of this book is not to answer all questions but merely to point the "way." The book should give you the stimulus necessary for studying karate as it should be studied. The stimulus was given to me by my karate teacher.

To explain briefly why I believe that karate is taught in this manner, I must first cover the physical qualities of karate. The movements and techniques, when learned openly, are not and cannot be mind-body reactions. Only when a technique is developed without your knowing it can it be applied with the principles necessary for true karate. The techniques learned openly are useful for ordinary self-defense, but they are not the real karate mind-body reflexes that karate masters are noted for. These reflexes can be developed only from within, without thought. The moment you become aware of their presence is the moment when you can apply them most efficiently.

This being the case then, which kata is all-in-all the most useful for true karate? The answer is this: the kata that appears to be the most simple—sanchin. Now we can complete the circle described earlier. When the student has mastered the openly applied techniques in san-ju-roku, he then can only go further by studying sanchin harder. When the student has become aware of all the openly applied techniques of seisan and san-ju-roku in sanchin, he has developed them to such a point that he can apply them, using mind-body directed reflexes. The student has completed the circle for the first time.

By this time, though, the student is an old man. But he is the possessor of a youthful and healthy body. His mind is keen and alert. He then begins to wonder. If all these techniques and movements which twenty years ago he thought were nonexistent are in the simple kata sanchin, then how many more techniques are still hidden in seisan and san-ju-roku? To sum up part of the philosophy of karate within a sentence, I need only say that the karate masters know the meaning of humility upon reaching this stage. To explain more would destroy the path that I have tried to point out. Karate is unexcelled as a way of life. Within the karate training lies what every human being needs most: a chance to find himself, by himself.

The kata circle or cycle can best be explained with an analogy. Think of the kata as a huge tree, sanchin being the roots and trunk, the other kata being the limbs, branches, and leaves. When a new tree is planted, or when sanchin is first learned, it does not appear to be what it really is. The seed does not look like a tree, nor do the movements of sanchin appear like karate in its entirety. If you wish to admire branches from a tree, you can cut them and arrange them prettily in a vase, but you must remember that these branches are cut off from their roots and are therefore technically dead, even though they look alive.

While you are nurturing sanchin, you become concerned with self-defense movements and more "advanced" kata. Your teacher shows you tricks and advanced kata, but they do nothing for you except to show you what the real thing looks like. The movements are just as dead as the branches that are cut off a tree. As your tree grows, however, and develops branches of its own, the tree becomes complete.

After the tree matures and develops blossoms of its own, it seeds. The seeds drop to the ground to be nurtured and developed into other trees. This resembles the circle or the cycle that the karate master goes through. Upon completing the first cycle of "meanings" and techniques, he begins to study all over again, developing a whole new "meaning" of sanchin through the restudy of the other kata.

The more kata you study, the larger is the circle, but the faster is the cycle. Those schools which develop many kata in an attempt to speed up the cycle actually do so, but many times the student becomes so concerned with the apparent techniques that he becomes content and confident, therefore actually slowing down the cycle.

■ How to learn seisan

Seisan, like sanchin, must be learned and studied in steps or stages. Listed below are the stages you should follow in developing the kata. Follow them carefully.

1. Break the kata down into six parts. Study it part by part until the whole kata is learned well.

2. Begin to go through the parts or stages of seisan, first doing two at a time, then three, etc., until finally you are performing the whole kata.

3. Go through the kata in slow motion at least twice a day. Then do it at regular speed.

While doing the kata, remember that the movements must be co-ordinated and smooth. The slow-motion movements are used in order to perfect the movements and techniques of the kata. Just as a moving picture of a fired bullet viewed in slow motion reveals the speed of the bullet to be constant and smooth, so too are the movements of the kata and all other karate movements. When the movements of the kata are performed in slow motion, the instructor can correct mistakes in form and technique—mistakes that could not easily be corrected if the kata was done at regular speed.

The arrows superimposed on the pictures show the direction of the movements. The foot chart under each picture shows the foot stance in which the movement should be performed and also shows the movement in relation to the previous movement. The movements composing a single technique are indicated by a single number.

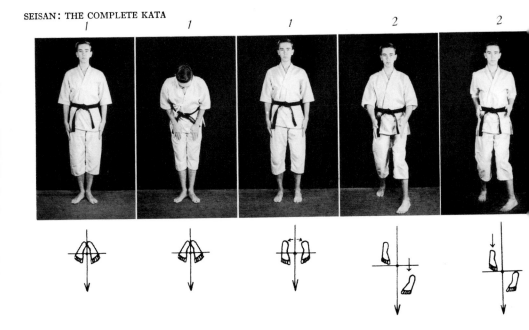

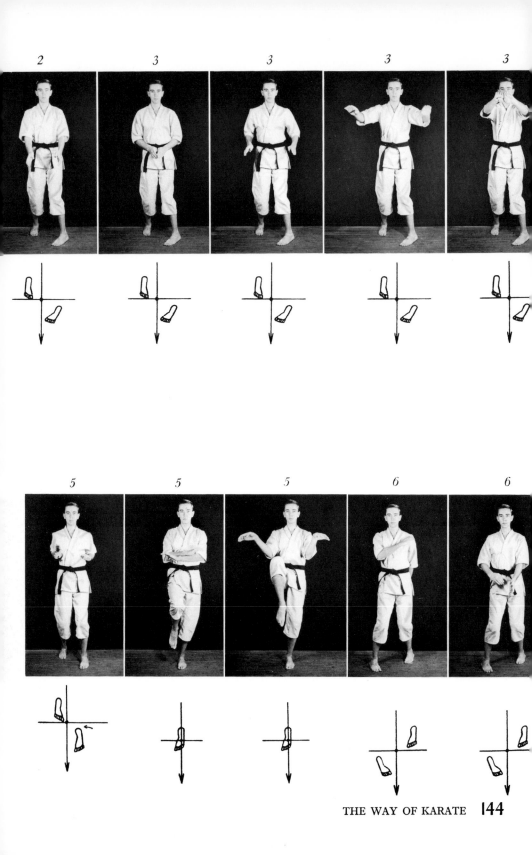

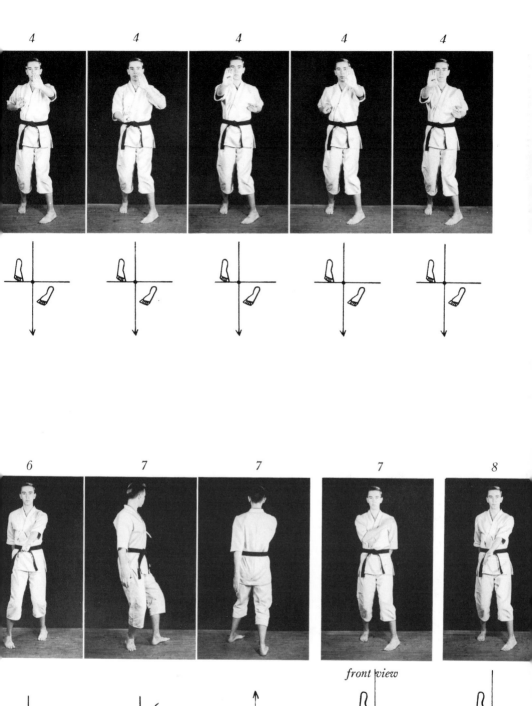

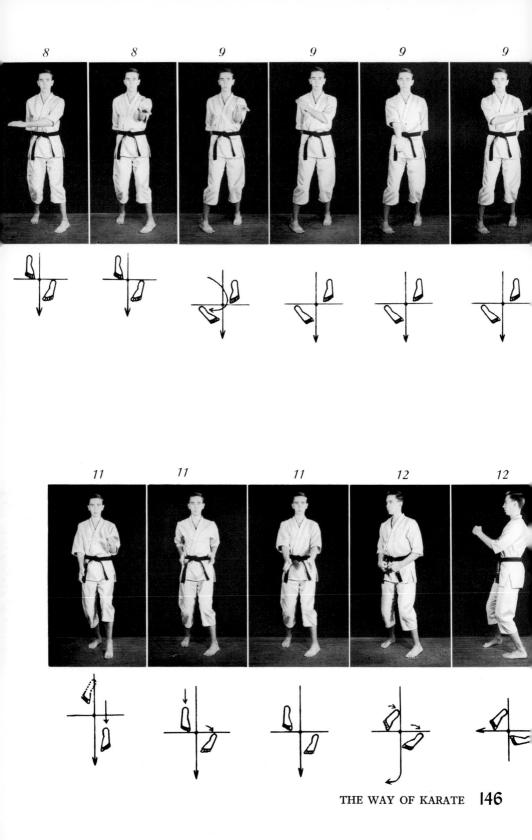

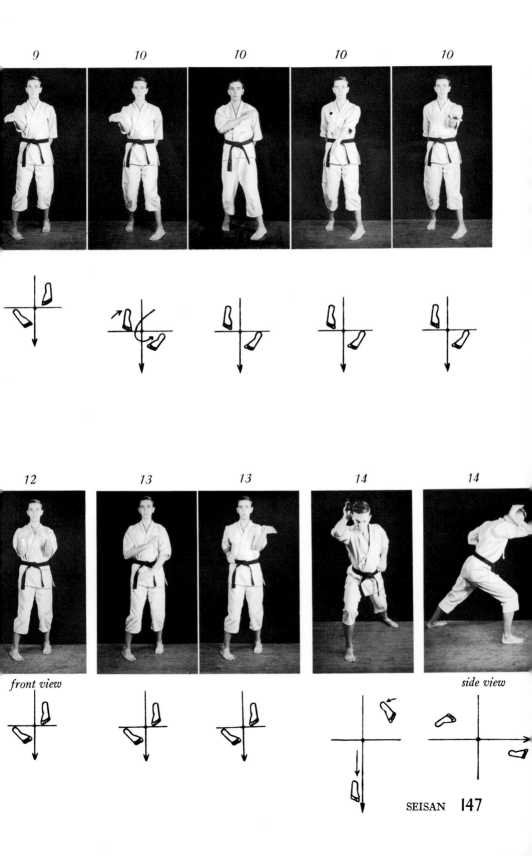

9   10   10   10   10

12   13   13   14   14

front view

side view

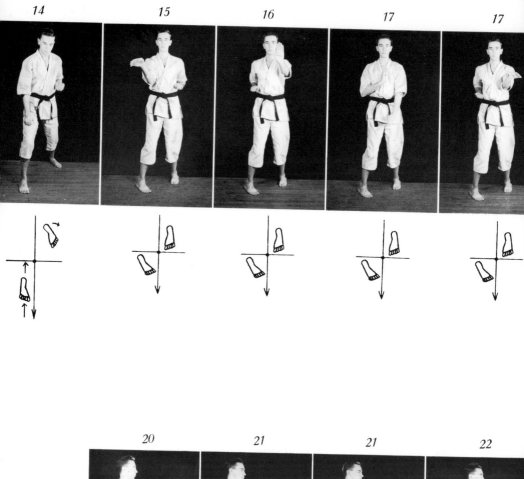

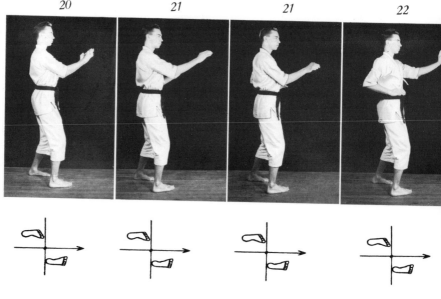

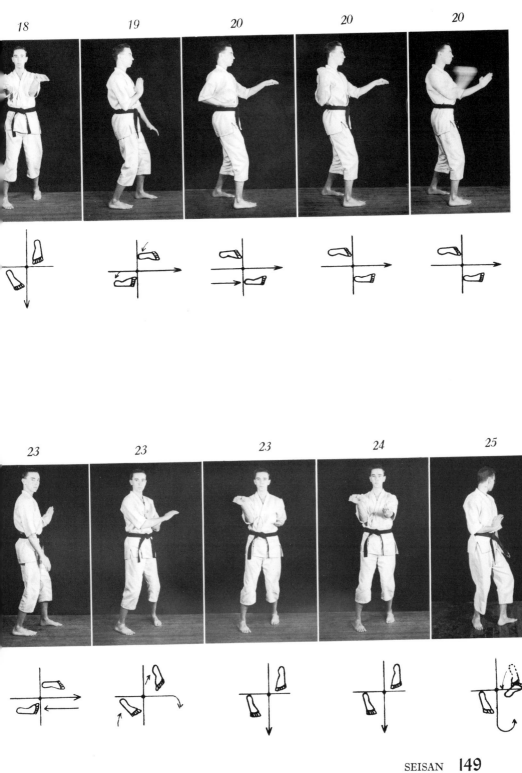

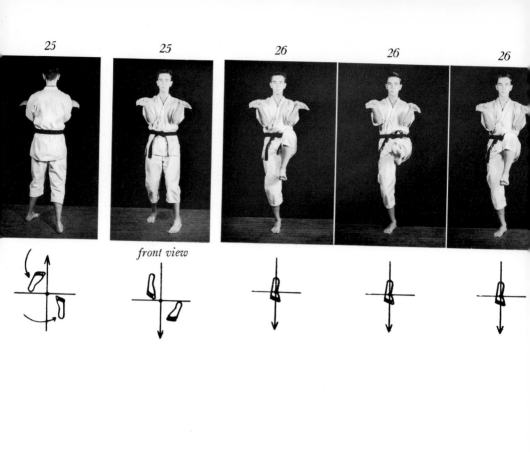

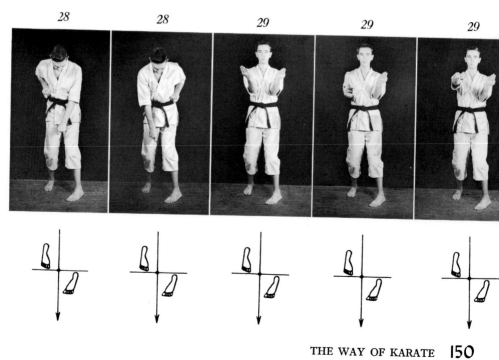

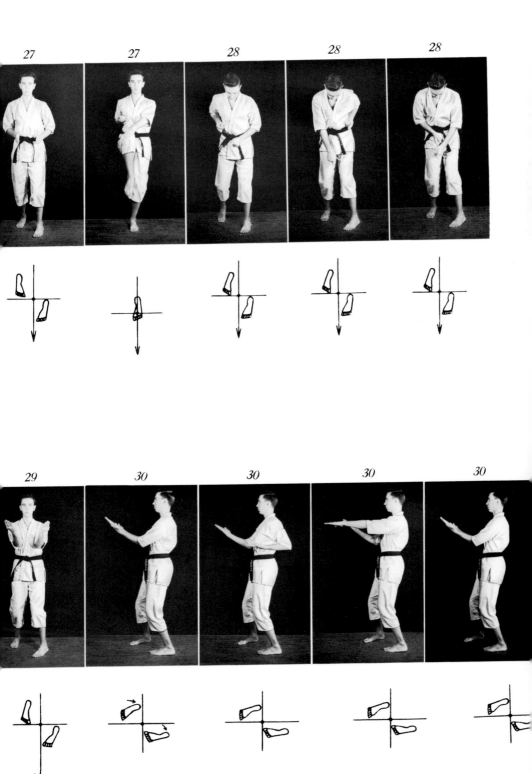

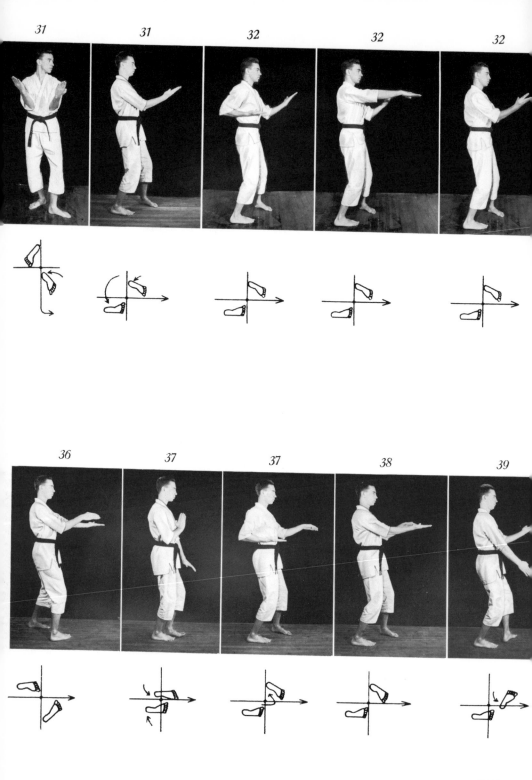

41   41   42   43   44

front view

47   47   48

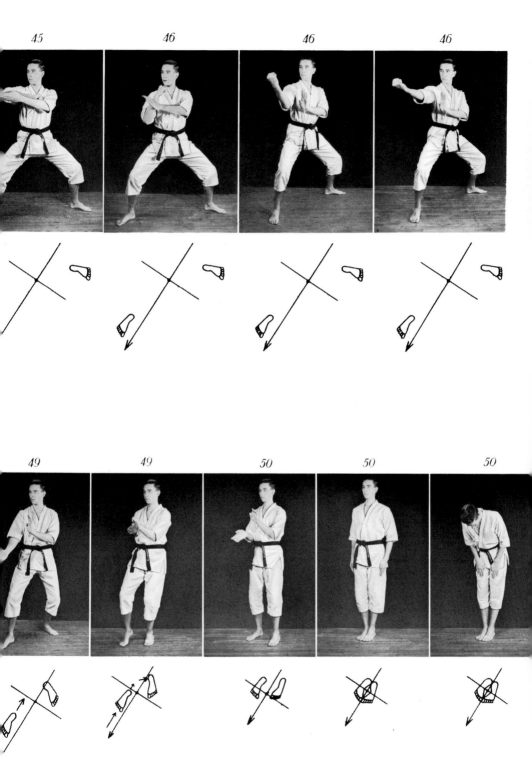

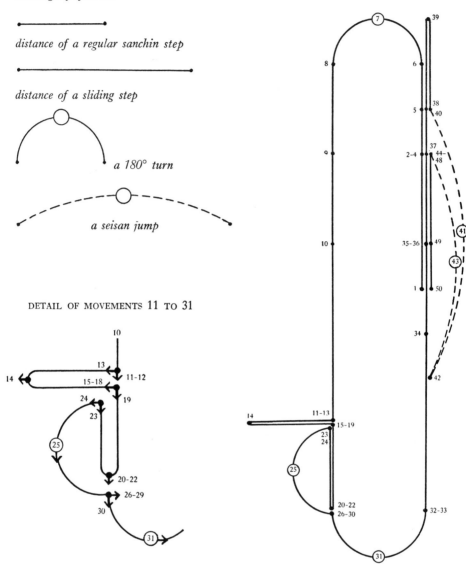

distance of a regular sanchin step

distance of a sliding step

a 180° turn

a seisan jump

DETAIL OF MOVEMENTS 11 TO 31

■ **Seisan over-all movement chart**

The over-all movement chart is designed to help the student who has learned the basic movements of seisan and who wishes to check his over-all movements for accuracy. A kata always begins and ends at the same point. This is one of the checks of the kata.

The chart, however, should not be taken as an accurate tracing of the actual movements as performed, but rather as a schematic presentation to help the student obtain a general idea of the over-all pattern of the exercise. The part corresponding to movements 11 to 31 is given in detail to show the shifts in the direction of the body.

■ Summary of seisan

The kata seisan can never be stressed enough. You should practice it faithfully at every workout along with sanchin. Through seisan you will be able to advance yourself, even though you do not have the guidance of a karate teacher. Do not stress speed in seisan but strive for accuracy and perfection. Once you have developed the movements of seisan, you will automatically have developed the speed and coordination necessary to perform any one of the techniques with speed and accuracy.

Use the diagrams faithfully whenever you practice the kata. Have your karate partner watch your movements and the corresponding movements from the book. Make corrections after each stage of seisan. When the kata has been learned well, practice the interpretation of seisan with your partner as in the fundamental sparring exercises. *As you progress, study your kata more and more, for in the kata lies the key to advanced karate training.*

I realize that you will have many questions about the kata and about your karate training in general that would be impossible to answer completely in a book of this size. If you are studying karate faithfully and have run up against an obstacle that seems insurmountable, write to me, and I will answer your questions if at all possible.

▪ 12

Elbow, Hand, and Wrist Strikes

■ The elbow and its use

The elbow is an effective weapon for close combat. When used properly, it can prove devastating to your opponent. You can learn the correct application of the elbow-strike from the elbow-striking exercise described in Chapter 3. Shown on the following two pages are three applications of this technique: block and counterattack from a low stance, block and counterattack from a leaningforward stance, and counterattack for a strangle hold.

ready-attack stance

*block and counterattack
(from low stance)*

IMPORTANT POINTS TO REMEMBER ABOUT THE ELBOW-STRIKE

1. Learn the basic elbow-strike by practicing the elbow-striking exercise.

2. Follow closely the "points to remember" about the exercise.

3. Practice the elbow-strike from various stances, using different blocks before striking; for example, the rising block with the left arm followed by an elbow-strike with the right arm.

4. Remember to keep your back and head straight throughout the technique.

5. When using the elbow-strike from a leaning-forward stance, remember to keep your body in a straight line with your rear leg.

ready-attack stance

*block and counterattack
(from leaning-forward stance)*

strangle hold   *counterattack*

6. The calf of your forward leg is perpendicular to the floor when the strike is completed.

7. The striking arm completes its strike as your body completes its downward movement into the leaning-forward stance.

8. Keep your shoulders facing straight ahead toward your opponent and parallel to the floor.

9. In situations where the forearm of the striking arm must act as a blocking agent, tighten the arm muscles as you strike by bending the hand forward.

■ **The hand and wrist: uses for blocking and striking**

The hand and wrist can be used in an infinite number of ways for blocking, for striking, and for combinations of both.

knife-hand strike

knife hand

palm heel   *one-knuckle fist*

■ **Palm-heel block (teisho-uke)**

This block, shown below at left, is developed from the wrist-blocking and fishtail-blocking exercises.

■ **Palm-heel pushing block (nagashi-uke)**

This block, shown above at right, is executed to the outside. As your opponent attacks, sidestep and push his thrusting arm outward.

■ **Bent-wrist block (kakuto-uke)**

This block, shown at left, is developed from the wrist-blocking exercise.

ELBOW, HAND, AND WRIST TECHNIQUES   **161**

■ **Combination block and strike (tsuki-uchi)**

This technique is executed by stepping into the attacking thrust. Bend your blocking elbow outward as you strike. This technique is developed from seisan.

■ **Knife-hand strike (shuto-uchi)**

This strike is developed from the kata seisan.

- **Ridge-hand and foreknuckle strike (haito-uchi and hiraken-uchi)**
  This strike is developed from the kata seisan.

- **Spear-hand strike (yonhon-nukite-uchi)**
  This strike is developed from seisan.

■ Back-fist strike (riken-uchi)

■ Summary

The striking techniques are fairly simple to understand. This does not mean that they are necessarily easy to learn. You must practice the striking techniques often to develop the reflexes needed to execute the movements properly.

The striking techniques illustrated are by no means a complete list, but they are the basic strikes from which others can be developed. Following is a check list from which you can check a technique that does not come from one of the two kata described in this book:

1. Does the technique violate any principle of sanchin (footwork, posture, arm movements, etc.)?

2. Does the technique do what another known technique does better? If so, forget it.

3. Can you move quickly from the technique into another?

4. Are you in a weak position while you are applying the technique? If so, it is wrong.

You should never use techniques that are not found in a recognized kata. All of the techniques in the book are found in the two kata, sanchin and seisan.

■ A question and its answer

Assuming that both are delivered with the same amount of power and speed, which is more effective, a thrust or a strike?

The strike is more effective, and therefore more dangerous. The strike makes contact with the same amount of speed and power, but the power is much more concentrated than in the thrust. A thrust makes contact over a larger surface than does a strike. The shock waves are more dispersed and therefore weaker. All of the power of the strike is concentrated within a small area, and the shock waves are more penetrating and deadly.

Since the strikes are more dangerous, refrain from using them in actual self-defense unless is it absolutely necessary.

.13

Sparring Techniques

■ Kihon-kumite: fundamental sparring

There are two ways in which the student develops the fundamentals of sparring. First, he defends himself against an attack toward a prearranged spot. He also knows which arm his partner will attack with. The second way is for him to defend himself against a random attack. He does not know where the attack is coming from or where it is going.

Shown on pages 168-69 are a few attacks and possible counterattacks that may be used for kihon-kumite. By studying the kata, the student can develop many more.

■ Explanations of kihon-kumite examples

1. Attacks with blocks
   a. ready-attack stance
   b. bent-wrist block (kakuto-uke)
   c. outside middle-area block (chudan-soto-uke)
   d. rising upper-area block (jodan-age-uke)
   e. downward block (gedan-barai)
   f. forearm block (ude-uke)
   g. hooking block to the outside (kake-uke)
   h. palm-heel pushing block (nagashi-uke)
   i. X block from a low stance (juji-uke)
2. Counterattacks
   j. front-snap foot-strike (mae-geri-keage)
   k. back-fist strike (riken-uchi)
   l. spear-hand strike (yonhon-nukite-uchi)
   m. elbow-strike (empi-uchi)

IMPORTANT POINTS TO REMEMBER ABOUT KIHON-KUMITE, PREARRANGED

1. Bow at the beginning and end of the series, not before and after each attack.

2. *Never* actually strike your partner. Always "pull" the thrust short of the target.

3. When thrusting, step forward as you deliver the thrust. The arm should stop as the feet stop.

4. Always step into a good stance. Make sure that the stance is strong for the technique performed.

5. For this technique, use the karate thrust developed in the karate thrusting exercise described in Chapter 7.

6. Keep your back and head straight and facing your partner throughout the sparring technique.

7. Do about 10 repetitions of each appropriate block for the following attacking techniques:
   a. low thrust—to the stomach
   b. middle thrust—to the solar plexus
   c. high thrust—to the head

8. Know all the basic blocks, thrusts, and foot-strikes well before attempting to learn the fundamental sparring exercise.

9. Use the principles of Zen in your sparring. Do not anticipate an attack or a movement. Wait a split second until you are sure of the attack; then trigger your defensive block.

KIHON-KUMITE EXAMPLES

ready-attack stance

attacks with eight examples of blocks

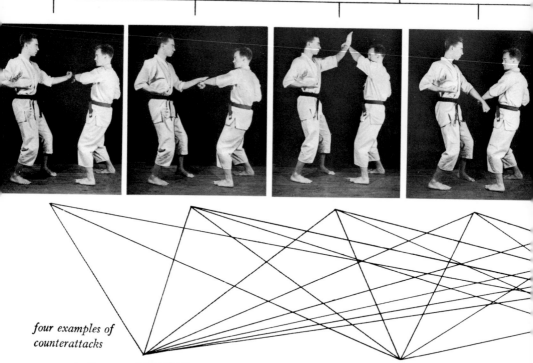

*four examples of
counterattacks*

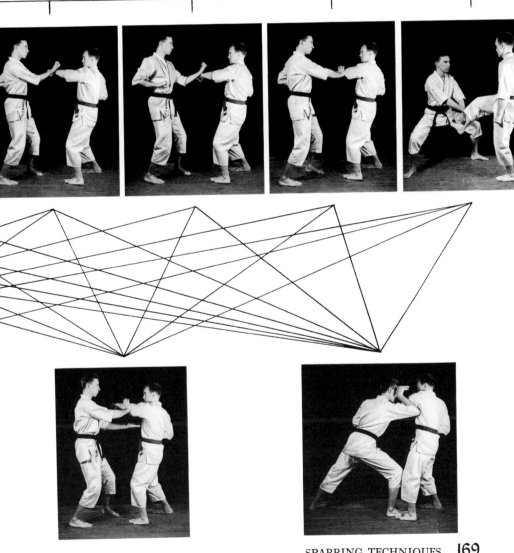

■ Fundamental sparring: random attack

After you have practiced the prearranged sparring exercise for about 10 sessions, you will be ready to advance into the random attacking techniques. The method of attack and defense is the same as in the prearranged exercise, except that the student who is defending himself does not know when the attack is coming or where it is directed.

Be especially careful in this exercise not to hit the person on the defensive. If your reflex action is slow or if you cannot stop a thrust where you want it to stop, work harder on the reflex-building exercise described in Chapter 7. A more advanced method of this exercise is to move about as if you were actually sparring. The attacker moves about looking for an opening. When he finds it, he delivers *one* thrust to the unprotected area. (He "pulls" the thrust, of course.) The defender moves about, keeping at least an arm-and-a-half length away from the attacker. When the person attacks, the defender blocks with an appropriate technique. A third party should be refereeing the match, watching for mistakes. At the end of a match, the referee tells the two participants what mistakes they have made.

After completing a match, the participants change roles, the defender becoming the attacker and vice versa. Do not use foot-striking techniques until you are capable of controlling them.

■ Summary of kihon-kumite principles

The student should keep in mind that if he should actually hit the student he is practicing with, serious injury could result. Because karate is new in America, people are going to be watching it closely. A serious injury through the carelessness of a karate student could damage the reputation of karate greatly. *Be careful.*

Through kihon-kumite, the student can test his blocks, thrusts, and foot-strikes against an opponent. This experience helps give the student confidence in his defensive ability. When the student becomes really good at karate, he will not doubt his abilities and will probably never get into a fight. A real karate student will be able to talk his way out of fights or walk away from them, because he does not have to prove to anyone (his friends or himself) that he can take care of himself. *He* knows he can, and that is all that matters. Only insecure persons start fights. Act like a real karate student right from the start. Use your brains whenever possible instead of your fists. Prove to yourself that you are a good karate student at the training sessions and not on the streets.

one of the apparent techniques in seisan being applied on an opponent

■ Competitive sparring

Sparring is a recent innovation in Okinawa. Prior to 1940 there was nothing in karate that could warrant its being called a sport. Some of the masters began to experiment by using various kinds of protective equipment that might be able to protect the body against a blow, but to no avail. Nothing short of a suit of armor could be used.

Finally someone reasoned that if the karate student's reflexes were keen enough to stop a blow wherever he desired, why could he not stop a thrust, foot-strike, or arm-strike short of contact while sparring? Experiments were successful from the start. The matches turned out to be extremely safe because of the rigid rules and regulations that governed them.

A test that all participants had to pass was to spar with an instructor or advanced student, using the instructor's outstretched hand as a target. The student had to strike, thrust, and foot-strike at the moving hand for three minutes, coming close to the hand but never touching it. The student very seldom attempted this test unless he had been studying karate for at least six months. During this test, the student would also be tested for correctness of technique. Very few students passed this test the first time. Once a student did begin sparring, however, he was never the cause of a sparring accident. I hope that you will adopt these same rigid standards.

■ Technique sparring

The first method of competitive sparring is for technique only. The winner does not win because he has scored the most effective blows but because he had demonstrated superior form in his blocks, thrusts, and foot-strikes.

This method of sparring is best to use in the beginning, because the student will be more concerned with scoring an attacking or a defending technique correctly than with just scoring a technique. In sparring with a student who is also inexperienced, you may be able to score an attack effectively even though it is sloppy, but this will not improve your over-all karate, nor will it help you in sparring with superior students.

Technique sparring may be performed by using thrusts alone at first for safety reasons. Or the judge may designate an area as a target zone—say the belt—to which all thrusts and foot-strikes are directed. As the student progresses, the target zone may be enlarged.

■ Advanced point sparring

Point sparring involves scoring a blow (short of contact) to any one of three scoring zones. These scoring zones are the head or neck, the chest, and the stomach. The effectiveness of these blows is to be determined by a referee. This type of sparring is very advanced, and I suggest that you do not begin it until after at least a year of training.

■ **Basic rules and regulations governing karate sparring matches, as used by the Okinawan masters**

1. The contest should be held in a circular area approximately 35 feet in diameter. The floor should be smooth.

2. The outside of the ring should be marked off with a light, easily seen border.

3. The referee should be an advanced student (for a new school) or an instructor.

4. The match will be five minutes in length for advanced students and one minute or more in length for students just beginning to spar.

5. The members of the class who are advanced students shall be the judges and shall be seated around the contest area.

6. For a sparring match that is to be judged on technique, the judges (advanced students) shall vote on a winner. The contestants shall not watch the voting. The contestant receiving a majority of the votes shall be declared the winner by the referee.

7. For advanced sparring, there shall be two referees. When a "killing" blow is detected, the referee seeing the blow stops the match and declares the contestant that delivered the blow the winner. The time limit for advanced sparring is five minutes. After that time, if no "killing" blow had been delivered, the advanced students shall judge the winner by technique, as in regulation number 6.

8. If at any time during the match the referee sees any *foul play* or unsportsmanlike behavior on the part of a contestant, he shall immediately declare him the loser. The decision of the referees shall be final.

9. Any rule that seems appropriate may be voted into effect by a two-thirds majority.

10. Begin and end the contest by bowing. Bow first to the chief instructor and then to the judges (advanced students).

■ Sparring stances

In this section are discussed a few of the many stances that can be used while sparring. Some are used because of the ease with which the student can block attacks from them. Others are used because attacks are quicker from them. I suggest that you learn and use them all. Do not stay in a stance too long. Change positions and stances often in order to confuse your opponent. Remain flexible throughout the match, being able to move from one technique to another quickly and easily. Spar as you would play a game of chess. Without actually thinking of combinations, develop your senses to respond to the weaknesses of your opponent. Learn to recognize poor moves and be able to capitalize on them. In order to become really proficient at sparring, you must apply all the karate principles in this book to your movements. Study sanchin in order to develop your focusing ability, seisan to develop defensive and counterattacking techniques.

1. BASIC SPARRING STANCE

The basic sparring position is simply a sanchin position. The only variation is that the palms of your hands are pointing downward. This position is equally strong for blocking and for attacking.

2. UECHI'S STANCE

This stance is used frequently by Mr. Uechi. It is extremely strong for blocking. The right arm is positioned nicely for fast, effective blocks, either for thrusts or foot-strikes. The left arm may be used effectively for fast wrist blocks, a favorite of Mr. Uechi.

3. RYUKO'S STANCE

This stance is the favorite of Ryuko Tomoyose because of its attacking possibilities. The left arm is strong for blocking, and the right arm is strong for attacking.

■ Summary

You will find sparring very interesting if you are careful. Not only can you test your techniques, but you can actually improve your over-all karate. You must be careful, though. Otherwise, a sparring match can turn into disaster.

The karate thrusts, foot-strikes, and arm-strikes are precision movements. If yours are not developed before you begin to spar, someone will definitely get hurt.

While sparring, practice all the principles learned in sanchin and seisan. Be relaxed but alert while watching for an opening or waiting for an attack. When you attack or deflect an attack, use your sanchin training to focus all the power of your body into the technique.

Never get too close to your opponent. Always keep an area of at least an arm and a half's length defended. When you attack, move in slightly—just enough so that your arm would reach your opponent if extended. Then attack, never bending your head or in any other way violating the laws of sanchin or seisan.

.14
Training Equipment, Classes, and Schedules

■ Training equipment

All the equipment you will need in the beginning is a cleared area. The floor should be smooth and very clean. When you begin the arm- and fist-strengthening stage, you will need a thrusting board or *makiwara*. This board is not to be used to callous the knuckles or to deform the hands. The makiwara is to be used to toughen the skin on the knuckles and arms and to build a slight cartilage along the striking surface of the hands, arms, and knuckles. This cartilage will in no way affect the movement of your arms, hands, or

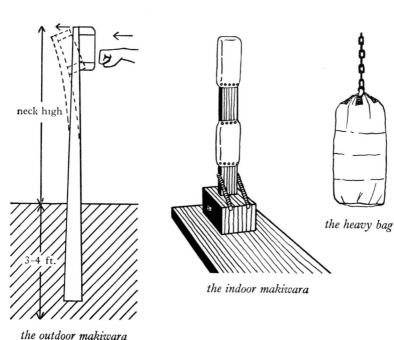

neck high

3–4 ft.

the outdoor makiwara

the indoor makiwara

the heavy bag

fingers. If you do not follow the correct method of training, however, and you injure yourself, you will regret it later by having stiff joints and possibly arthritis.

If you have a place outdoors to put the makiwara, it should look like the one shown on the opposite page. The striking surface of the board can be either grass rope (the grass heals any abrasions quickly) or sponge rubber.

Your training should be very slow at first, because your body is not used to this type of conditioning. Massage your arm and hand muscles after each session. After one year's training with the makiwara, limit your training sessions to one a week.

The indoor makiwara (opposite page) can be made as elaborate as time and money permit.

The heavy bag (opposite page) is used for thrusting and for foot-striking. It can be made of canvas or leather and can be stuffed with rubber scraps or rags. Be sure that you use *good* karate thrusts, strikes, and foot-strikes whenever you use the heavy bag.

The stretching bar is used to stretch the leg muscles. Keep the leg that is being stretched relaxed in order to get results.

■ Suggestions on developing a karate class

You can learn karate on your own, but you can learn it much more easily if you are part of a group. One person cannot correct his own mistakes, nor can he do the exercises involving two persons. Here are some suggestions which you might follow in setting up a small group and eventually a class.

A good place to begin training is a Y.M.C.A. Such organizations usually have the facilities necessary to begin a class. The most important ingredient needed for your class is a nucleus of men who have good character and are hard workers. You will want men who are good organizers and fast learners. Later, when the members of this nucleus have progressed to a point where they can teach, you can take slower learners.

Begin your class as a study group. Devote the full workouts to studying from the book. Learn the correct terminology and use it during the workout. Study the two kata and take turns going through them while the other members watch for various mistakes.

One can watch the footwork, another the arm movements, etc. Spend at least three or four months studying within this study group, and do not take any new students during this time.

When the members of the group feel that they have reached a level where they are all familiar with everything in the book, hold an election. Elect as chief instructor the man who has shown the most progress in the kata and in the karate attitude. He should be elected only because he is superior in his karate attitude and ability, not because he is the most popular.

When the group has decided on a chief instructor, have him lead the exercises and formal karate workout. Study together for another three months. Then, if you wish, open the class to new students. Be very careful in selecting new members. Your concern should be with quality rather than quantity. Your class will grow more slowly, but it will gain a better reputation because of its selectiveness.

As the class grows, the head instructor should appoint assistant instructors to help teach. The number of assistant instructors should be in proportion to the number of students in the class. The basic group should number about five. The group should never have more than five students to an assistant instructor. The chief instructor's decisions should be final in all matters not covered in the book. If further advice is wanted, however, you may correspond with me. I will attempt to help you as much as possible.

The workouts should be held at least six times a week in the beginning and never less than three times a week after the class has been completely organized. The Mattson Karate Academy has workouts available six times a week for two hours. The students then work out on their own at home, practicing the techniques learned at the academy. Following is a suggested workout schedule to be used during the first stage of your karate training.

TRAINING SCHEDULE, FIRST MONTH

(6 sessions per week)

1. All exercises in Chapter 3.
2. Bowing ceremony.
3. Learn and study sanchin, part one.
4. Learn and study the foot-striking techniques, 15 repetitions each.

5. Learn and study the blocking techniques, 15 repetitions each.

6. Learn and study the thrusting exercises.

7. Learn and study kake.

8. Do about 5 loosening-up exercises (Chapter 3).

9. Relax for at least an hour before taking a shower. The Okinawan masters give themselves rubdowns with a coarse towel after a workout and then wait at least two hours before taking a shower.

TRAINING SCHEDULE, SECOND AND THIRD MONTHS (6 sessions per week)

1. All exercises.

2. Bowing ceremony.

3. Develop sanchin, part one. (Remain "soft" while performing the kata.)

4. Foot-striking techniques, 15 repetitions each.

5. Blocking techniques, 15 repetitions each.

6. Thrusting exercise, 50 repetitions.

7. Thrusting techniques, 20 repetitions.

8. Kake and arm-strengthening exercise.

9. Learn and study the sparring exercise.

10. Learn and do the arm- and fist-strengthening exercise—10 minutes of training.

11. Loosening-up exercises.

12. Rubdown, relax, and shower.

TRAINING SCHEDULE, FOURTH AND FIFTH MONTHS (6 sessions per week)

1. All exercises.

2. Bowing ceremony.

3. Sanchin, with part two.

4. Foot-striking techniques, 15 repetitions each.

5. Blocking techniques, 15 repetitions each.

6. Thrusting exercise, 50 repetitions.

7. Thrusting techniques, 20 repetitions.

8. Kake and arm-strengthening exercise.

9. Sparring exercise, 5 repetitions.

10. Learn and study seisan.

11. Develop fundamental sparring techniques.

12. Arm- and fist-strengthening exercise, 15 minutes.

13. Loosening-up exercises.

14. Rubdown, relax, and shower.

TRAINING SCHEDULE, PERMANENT

1. All exercises.

2. Bowing ceremony.

3. Three complete sanchin, with focusing.

4. Foot-striking techniques, 10 repetitions each.

5. Blocking techniques, 10 repetitions each.

6. Blocking and foot-striking combinations (three or more combinations of a block and a foot-strike), 10 repetitions each.

7. Thrusting exercise, 50 repetitions.

8. Block-and-thrust combinations (three or more combinations of a block and a thrust), 10 repetitions each.

9. Kake and arm-strengthening exercise.

10. Sparring exercise, 10 repetitions.

11. Three seisan, all done slowly.

12. Fundamental sparring techniques (low, high, and middle attacks).

13. Loosening-up exercises.

14. Rubdown, relax, and shower.

Once a month, when students are ready, leave out techniques 6, 8, 9, and 12. The end of the workout can be devoted to free-style sparring.

■ A word of caution

Be especially careful in starting your class, making sure that you get men who are going to stick with it and will not give karate a bad name by getting into trouble. Remember that karate is quite new in America and that people will be watching your group closely. You can either make karate a respected name or confirm people's beliefs that it is a dangerous weapon used by crazy men.

■ Karate for women

Karate may be studied by women for purposes of self-defense and physical conditioning. Size is of no great importance in karate, so a woman can learn it nearly as well as a man. The women I have taught so far have actually picked up the movements faster than many of the male students. Their bodies seem to be much more elastic, making the techniques easier to learn. The exercises and kata are very good for developing co-ordination and muscle tone. The defensive techniques, although not as effective as the men's, will stop any attacker.

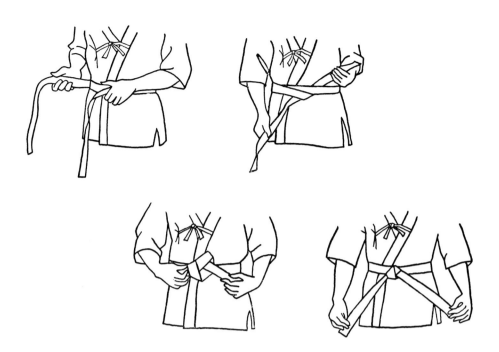

■ Karate uniform and belt system

The uniform used in karate is called a karate-gi. Its chief feature is the ceremonial belt, the proper tying of which is shown in the pictures (above). The belt is the symbol of a student's proficiency in karate. Belts can be awarded only by a recognized branch of the Okinawan Karate Association or the Japan Karate Association. Every new student is entitled to wear the white belt until he is promoted. The chart illustrates the ten grades of the belt through which the student progresses before being awarded the black belt. The student who trains at least three times weekly and progresses normally attains each belt in the time indicated.

The ten grades of belt before the black belt are temporary. The black-belt ratings are permanent but may be revoked if the holder commits a serious infraction of rules. The temporary status of a pre-black belt holder means that if a student should discontinue his training before attaining the black belt his present rating will be revoked after a six-month waiting period. Since only a black belt holder has sufficient knowledge and understanding of karate to enable him to study

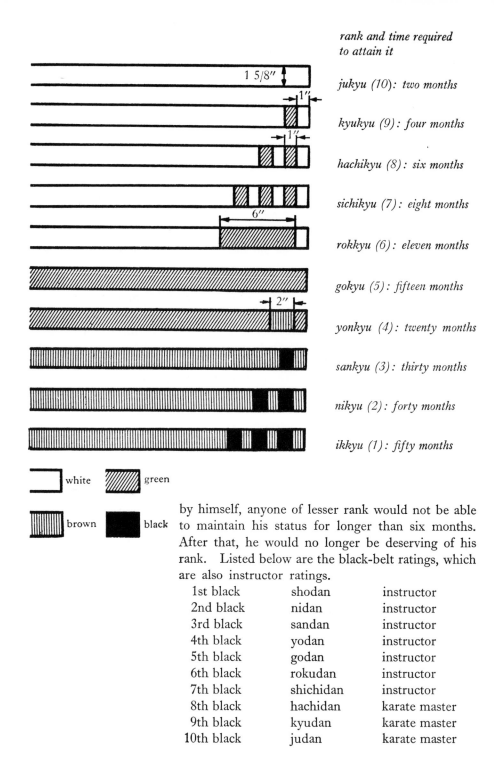

rank and time required to attain it

jukyu (10): two months

kyukyu (9): four months

hachikyu (8): six months

sichikyu (7): eight months

rokkyu (6): eleven months

gokyu (5): fifteen months

yonkyu (4): twenty months

sankyu (3): thirty months

nikyu (2): forty months

ikkyu (1): fifty months

1 5/8″   1″   1″   6″   2″

white   green   brown   black

by himself, anyone of lesser rank would not be able to maintain his status for longer than six months. After that, he would no longer be deserving of his rank. Listed below are the black-belt ratings, which are also instructor ratings.

1st black	shodan	instructor
2nd black	nidan	instructor
3rd black	sandan	instructor
4th black	yodan	instructor
5th black	godan	instructor
6th black	rokudan	instructor
7th black	shichidan	instructor
8th black	hachidan	karate master
9th black	kyudan	karate master
10th black	judan	karate master

THE WAY OF KARATE   182

.15

Legends of Karate

Until the present time there has been very little written about karate. All of the history was passed down from master to student by word of mouth. Much of the history was in the form of stories. Some of these stories had a moral behind them while others simply related experiences of the masters in China. Many times the masters would tell a story to clear up a certain point or to stress an important point. Following are some of the stories that were told to me while I was studying karate in Okinawa.

■ The Old Man and the Tiger

When Mr. Uechi, Sr., was studying karate in China sixty years ago, the Chinese people had few ways of protecting themselves other than with their bare hands. Because the people were relatively helpless in an emergency, they depended upon the karate masters for protection. The village karate master was called upon in any situation that would require someone with authority.

Mr. Uechi and his teacher were training one evening at home when a group of farmers from the outskirts of the village hurried to tell the teacher of their latest trouble. A huge man-eating tiger had come down from the mountains and was killing the livestock. The farmers pleaded with the teacher to help them kill the tiger. Mr. Uechi believed that the teacher was too old to attempt such a feat, so he volunteered himself for the job.

When Mr. Uechi said that he would go alone to slay the tiger, the teacher said that the task would require two men and he too would go. That night they set out to deal with the tiger.

At daybreak they arrived at the spot where the tiger had last struck. Mr. Uechi tied a small lamb to a post, and then the two men stood back to back about three feet from the lamb to begin their wait for the tiger. The teacher appeared calm and ready, but Mr. Uechi was a bit upset at the thought of the huge man-eating tiger lurking somewhere in the woods. The plan was to remain until the tiger attacked the lamb. The two men would then attempt to kill the tiger by striking it in the heart with a knuckle strike. Being back to back, the two men would not fall victim to a surprise attack. The day passed slowly, and both men grew quite weary. Mr. Uechi was now afraid that he would be too tired to fight the tiger if it attacked.

Suddenly they heard a movement in the woods. As it came closer, Mr. Uechi immediately became ready. He assumed a sanchin stance and prepared himself for the attack. Instead of a tiger, an old man with a flowing white beard walked into the clearing. He asked the two men why they were standing as they were. The teacher told the old man about the tiger and advised him to find a place of protection until it was killed.

The old man smiled and said that he had killed the tiger a short time before. He pointed back toward the woods in the direction from which he had come. Mr. Uechi and the teacher thought the old man was crazy, for how could an old man possibly kill a tiger that was three times as large as he?

Mr. Uechi asked the old man his name, and the old man started to walk away, detecting the sarcasm and disbelief in the tone of Mr. Uechi's voice. Mr. Uechi again asked the old man his name. This time the old man turned and said: "Never mind what my name is." Saying this, he walked into the woods.

The two men walked into the woods in the direction that the old man had indicated. About a quarter of a mile along the path they came to a clearing. Both men stared in amazement, for on the ground lay the dead tiger, just as the old man had said. The men examined the animal for weapon marks but could find none. Mr. Uechi turned the tiger over and saw that the animal's back had left an impression in the ground an inch deep.

The two men only guessed at what had happened, but it seemed sure that the tiger's back had been broken. Apparently the tiger had jumped the old man from the rear, and he had grabbed the animal's fore-feet and thrown it over his shoulder, snapping its back as he did. The deep imprint in the ground indicated that the old man must have possessed great strength and speed.

Mr. Uechi believed that the old man was a monk and a great karate master from another province. Neither Mr. Uechi nor his teacher ever saw him or heard of him again.

■ The Bluff

When karate was at its height in China about two hundred years ago, there was much rivalry among the masters. Usually the teachers would remain in their own districts and would not attempt to set up schools where another karate master was already teaching, but this was not always the case.

A young karate student who was exceptionally good at karate believed that he was better than any master and was set to prove it. He decided to take a trip to a nearby province where an old master was teaching. The young man knew that the only way he could prove to himself that he was tougher than the master was to fight him. The young man also knew it was next to impossible to provoke a master into a fight, so he devised a plan which he believed would make the master angry enough to fight.

The master lived at the top of a hill in a small home with his wife and three children. The season was fall, and the master and his family had just completed working in his garden, picking beans. The master was drying the beans on a blanket of grass on both sides of a path at the side of his house. The arrogant student believed that he could provoke the master into a fight by the following plan. He would carry a pole long enough to extend over both sides of the path along-side the master's house and would carry buckets filled with manure at both ends of the pole. When he reached the master's house, he would jostle the pole enough to spill the manure over the master's beans. "This," thought the student, "will surely get the master fighting mad, and then I will show him who is stronger."

When the student reached the master's house, he began to shake the manure over the master's beans and succeeded in making the master come running from his house. "What are you doing?" exclaimed the master. "Do you not realize that my family and I must eat these beans that you are so thoughtlessly ruining?"

"Yes, I realize that," said the student, "but I will continue to do what I am doing because you are not man enough to stop me."

The master smiled to himself, knowing now that this overconfident young man was a karate student who had not been trained properly and was now trying to prove his ability by fighting with him.

When the master smiled at the student, the student became enraged. "Why are you afraid to fight me?" he asked. "Are you afraid that you will lose respect in your village, or is it that you are just afraid?"

The master still said nothing but again smiled at the student.

The young man, now in a frenzy, dropped the buckets from the pole and held the pole in front of the master, saying that he was stronger than any man in China. He twisted the pole with all his might until it broke. He then threw the broken pole at the master's feet, saying: "You had better leave this area immediately, because I am going to start teaching karate here. You are an old man and should feel lucky that I do not beat you up before making you leave."

The master did not say a word but turned around and walked into the house. The student was elated that he had won this battle with a karate master who had the reputation of being one of the greatest masters in China. He felt that his surely proved that he was the strongest man in China.

The student was surprised when he saw the master come back carrying a large bamboo pole twice the size of the one he had just broken. The old man smiled as he offered the pole to the student, saying: "You are a strong young man. You have impressed me so much with your strength that I feel you will be able to break this pole also."

The student took the pole and began to twist it. He

twisted with all his might, but to no avail. For fifteen minutes he tugged, twisted, and pulled. He finally gave up, exhausted. He dropped the pole to the ground, saying that it was an impossible task. No human being could break this pole.

No sooner had the words been said than the old man picked up the pole and, with a tremendous twist, broke it in two. He smiled as he gave the two pieces to the young man and said: "Go back to your master and tell him to train your mind as well as he has trained your body. Then come back to visit me as a friend when you are able to duplicate this senseless feat of strength, so that we may smile together over your youthful and unwise act." The master then turned and walked back to his home and family.

The student went back to his master and began to study karate as the old man had advised.

■ The Lesson

Many of the stories of karate relate incidents concerning young men who had the wrong idea of karate. In these stories the young men usually learn a lesson in conduct and in respect.

A young man who had been studying karate for three years began using his knowledge to terrorize the people of a nearby village. Every week he would go into this village and bully people by pushing them around or beating them up if they resisted him in any way.

One afternoon while he was making his rounds of the taverns and market places of the village, he happened to bump into an old man who was stooped with age. The old man nearly fell over. Instead of helping him to his feet, the boy turned to the old man and said: "Why don't you watch where you are going? Do you not know better than to bump into me?"

The old man told him that he should be more respectful of his elders and should not be such a bully. At this the young man began to shout abuses and threats at the old man. He told him that he was crazy and stupid.

The old man was standing now, and he was again in the young man's path. The boy yelled at him again, telling him to get out of his way. The old man, however, told him that he should help him to this destination rather than ask him to move aside. At this the boy nearly exploded. He grabbed the old man, saying that he would teach him to respect the strong and that when he had finished with him the old man would know better than to ever talk back to him again.

There followed a one-sided battle in which the young man believed that he was nearly killing the old man. Punches and kicks flew to all parts of the old man's body until finally he was lying still on the ground. The boy was jubilant, for the old man had been able to strike him only once near the heart with a weak blow. So light was the blow that he could hardly feel it. The boy left the spot where the old man was lying and returned to his village.

A group of people who had witnessed the incident rushed to the old man and offered to help him, but he got up without any help, stood up straight, and walked briskly to his home.

About two weeks after the incident, the boy began to feel strange. He felt nauseated after all his meals, and he could not sleep well. After five weeks, he could not hold anything in his stomach. By the end of six weeks he had lost twenty pounds and was nearly dead. He then knew that the old man had done this to him. He now realized that what he had done was wrong, and he wished that he could be forgiven by the old man. Feeling certain that he was going to die, the boy sent his brother to search for the old man.

The old man had left word in the town of his whereabouts, as if he knew that the boy would try to contact him. The boy's brother found him the next day. Together they went to the boy's home.

When the boy saw the old man, he begged forgiveness for all the things he had done. The old man, seeing that the boy was truly sorry, told him that he would help his condition. He gave the boy some liquid to drink, and soon after that the boy was asleep. In a week he was on his feet again and feeling much better.

The old man then told the boy that the village people had sent for him from another district to cope with the young man. He also told the boy that he was a karate teacher. The boy immediately begged the old man to take him as student. The old man accepted him, and the boy became his best student.

■ Mr. Uechi, Sr. and the Bandits

Shortly before Mr. Uechi, Sr., came back to Okinawa, he went to visit all of his friends. On one such visit, which took him deep into a wooded area infested with bandits, he found occasion to use his karate.

When it came time for Mr. Uechi to return home, the hour was late. His friend urged him to stay the night because of the dangerous bandits that lurked along the path. Mr. Uechi had to be in his village the following morning, so he had to decline the invitation.

Walking along the wooded path, he was confronted by five bandits who demanded all his money. "I have no money, kind sirs, so please let me pass," said Mr. Uechi.

The leader of the bandits, a burly, rough-looking fellow, said: "If you have no money, we will take your clothes." Mr. Uechi replied that he would need his clothes to protect him from the insects on his way home.

Hearing this, the leader was furious. "I am a karate expert and am very strong," he said. "You had better take your clothes off and do it quickly, or I will punish you severely." Again Mr. Uechi refused, and the bandit, enraged, rushed at him.

Mr. Uechi calmly deflected the powerful thrust and counterattacked with a blow that instantly killed the bandit. Looking at the other bandits, he said: "Come and pick up your leader and dispose of him. I think this is great sport. Are there any more of you who wish to take my clothes?"

There was no response, so Mr. Uechi continued: "I will travel this district every night from now on in hopes of amusing myself. The next time, do not tell me of your whereabouts. Jump me silently from behind so that you do not make defending myself so easy." Mr. Uechi then walked home.

Every night for a week he walked the road to his friend's home, but he met with no further trouble. In fact, the area had no trouble with bandits for many years after.

Mr. Uechi, Sr., studied karate as hard as any other person in China while he was there. He loved the exercises and movements, but most of all he enjoyed doing sanchin. His Chinese instructor told him that through sanchin training he would be able to perform feats of strength with his body that would appear to be impossible. He studied sanchin diligently from the time that he began his training in 1900 until he died in 1947 at the age of seventy-nine. He returned to Okinawa and demonstrated some of these amazing feats which new students of karate find hard to believe possible.

■ Tests of Stability

Mr. Uechi performed these feats not to show how strong he was but to prove to his students that the human body has not so many limitations as most people believe it to have. He wanted to stress the importance of sanchin by doing feats which he said required no other training except sanchin.

The first feat he demonstrated was the stability test. He asked two of his largest and strongest students to pick up a large bamboo pole hanging over the door to his school and place it against his stomach. He then positioned himself in a sanchin stance and requested the two students to push as hard as they could. They did so for a minute or two, but they were unable to budge Mr. Uechi an inch.

There were no tricks involved in this feat. Mr. Uechi loved karate too much to have degraded it with trickery of any sort. He told his students that they could all duplicate the feat if they perfected sanchin to a high degree. Mr. Uechi, Jr., believes that the feat was performed by controlling the stomach muscles to such an extent that all the power of the men pushing the pole was absorbed by his body. No one knows for sure. The pole still hangs over the door, waiting for someone else to duplicate the feat.

After another workout, Mr. Uechi instructed his wife to bring him six fragile china teacups. He arranged these six cups about twelve inches apart in a straight line. He then instructed his smallest student, who weighed about ninety pounds, to walk from one cup to another until he had walked on all six cups.

The student placed his foot on the first cup, slowly putting his weight on it. Immediately the cup shattered. Mr. Uechi told him to try another cup—any cup along the line. The student broke the third cup in the row after trying to place his weight on it.

Mr. Uechi instructed his wife to bring out two more cups to replace the broken ones. He then placed his right foot on the first cup, putting all his weight on it. The cup did not break. Then he walked in a sanchin position from cup to cup, not breaking a single cup. He told his students that they also could learn to do this if they studied sanchin enough.

APPENDIX

Karate and Health

by Dr. Marvin Solit

A person who wishes to participate in a physical activity has hundreds of sports and games from which to choose. What are the special attributes of karate which set it apart from other physical activities? Why choose karate?

The answer to these questions raises a more fundamental question. Why engage in physical activity at all?

There are several reasons which motivate and justify our interest in sports and athletic activities. Of these, the one which most directly concerns physicians would be the improvement of physical health by building up strength and endurance and helping to prevent disease.

A closer examination of the facts, however, will reveal discrepancies between some of these properly accepted theories and other well-substantiated data, particularly in regard to athletic activities and health improvement. Popular opinion notwithstanding, extensive studies by physicians, life insurance companies, public health groups, etc., in which athletes or persons engaging in regular athletic activity were compared with their nonathletic cousins, disclose the following:

1.   The athlete's life span is not longer than that of the nonathlete, and, in fact, after the fiftieth year the nonathlete has a better record of longevity.

2.   Athletes do not have better resistance to infectious diseases, nor do they have faster recoveries from them, than nonathletes.

3.   Athletes do not show a lesser incidence in the number and severity of the "chronic degenerative" diseases—the diseases associated with the body's aging process.

It has been established, however, that athletic activities can lower the blood pressure, slow down the heart, promote increased circulation, increase muscle tone, and harden the body. We can understand this seeming paradox if we think of the human body as a machine—perhaps the most complicated and sophisticated of machines but still operating under and conforming to some of the same physical principles as man's less complicated machines.

If the wheels of your automobile were improperly aligned or unbalanced, resulting in excessive wear on the tires, axles, bearings, and chassis, would you try to correct the problem by simply driving the car or by increasing the driving time and speed? Obviously not. But when the parts of the human machine are not mechanically aligned (and over 99% of the population have faulty body mechanics), this is precisely what we do when we exercise. As the wheels and bearings of the automobile are subject to increased and uneven wear and tear, so are certain joints, muscles, organs, and tissues of the human body subject to excess and uneven usage. This helps explain why, from merely engaging in physical activity, we do not automatically reap the benefits of improved physical health. Only when the automobile and the human body are *correctly aligned* and *properly used* can they give maximum functioning efficiency and longevity.

Continuing our analogy, just as a smooth-running automobile must be driven to prevent carbon build-up, rust, and mechanical failures, the human body must be exercised to promote circulation and prevent stiffness and weakening of muscles and joints. The popular statement, "Exercise is healthful," must be modified to "Exercise is healthful if the body is used correctly."

Further reason for the athlete's poor health record is the higher incidence of accidents and residual damage to the body in the athletic group. The patient's statement, "That problem goes back to a school-day injury," is familiar to most physicians. A less recognized sequela of injury is the mechanical compensation that the body undergoes to avoid using the painful or damaged area. These compensations lower the functional level of the body and later lead to problems in areas remote from the site of the original trauma. In addition, many athletic activities use special and repeated patterns of motion which result in an overbalance of muscles and general limitations of motion, as in golf, bowling, pitching, etc.

Many athletic activities, by virtue of their strenuous nature, put too much strain on the body of the aging athlete. Much of the "fun" of his particular sport is lost as the athlete becomes older. As a result, either he gives up his sport and is then left with no activity when his health needs are greatest or he continues in his chosen sport and overburdens his body, as in such activities as weight lifting, handball, football, and track.

An activity that emphasizes and teaches correct use of the body, that is safe, and that can be enjoyed and participated in at every age, would obviate these points. Karate fits this description. Keeping in mind the human body's need for athletic activities, we return to our original question: "Why choose karate?" The answer can be given in four parts.

1. As a sport, karate offers all the pleasure, excitement, and satisfaction of a competitive sport without the risk of bodily injury. A student is not allowed to compete in karate matches until he has demonstrated his self-control; that is, his ability to stop his blows just before actual bodily contact with his opponent. Injuries are rare in karate.

2. Karate uses all the muscles of the body and produces balanced and symmetrical muscle development. In contrast with many physical activities that emphasize the development of a hard, tough body, karate masters wisely point out that a hard, tough body is not necessarily a healthy body. All exercise in karate is designed to develop an elastic body with muscles that are generally soft and supple but can instantly become steel-like when necessary. This concept is beautifully expressed in the words of Lao-tzu: "Man when living is soft and tender; when dead he is hard and tough. All animals and plants are tender and fragile; when dead they become withered and dry. Therefore it is said, the hard and the tough are parts of death; the soft and tender are parts of life. This is why the soldiers when they are too tough cannot carry the day; the tree when it is too tough will break. The position of the strong and great is low, and the position of the weak and tender is high."

3. Karate emphasizes and teaches posture correction and correct use of the body.

4. Karate can be adapted to suit both sexes and all ages. On the island of Okinawa many of the people participate in karate. It is a proven fact that these people live longer and healthier lives than those Okinawans who do not participate in karate.

Index